Wordsworth
Now and Then

Wordsworth Now and Then

Romanticism and contemporary culture

ANTONY EASTHOPE

Open University Press
Buckingham · Philadelphia

Open University Press
Celtic Court
22 Ballmoor
Buckingham
MK18 1XW

and
1900 Frost Road, Suite 101
Bristol, PA 19007, USA

First published 1993

A catalogue record of this book is available from the British Library

ISBN 0 335 09460 0 (pb) 0 335 09461 9 (hb)

Typeset by Colset Private Ltd, Singapore
Printed in Great Britain by St Edmundsbury Press Ltd,
Bury St Edmunds, Suffolk

I'm in words, made of words, others' words

Samuel Beckett

Contents

Dates

1770 William Wordsworth born 7 April, Cockermouth, Cumberland, second son of John Wordsworth, lawyer.

1778 Mother dies; William enters Hawkshead Grammar School.

1783 Father dies, being owed large debts; children placed in guardianship of uncles.

1787 Enters St John's College, Cambridge.

1791 BA.

1793 *An Evening Walk, Descriptive Sketches.*

1795 Inherits £900 from friend, Raisley Calvert, and settles with sister Dorothy at Racedown in Dorset; meets Coleridge.

1797 Moves to Alfoxden to be nearer Coleridge at Nether Stowey in Dorset.

1798 Wordsworth and Coleridge publish *Lyrical Ballads* anonymously ('The Ancient Mariner' is by Coleridge, the rest, including the 'Tintern Abbey' poem, are by Wordsworth); Wordsworth, Coleridge and Dorothy visit Germany.

1799 William and Dorothy settle in Dove Cottage, Grasmere.

1800 Second edition of *Lyrical Ballads* published under name of 'W. Wordsworth' with additional poems (including 'Lucy' poems) and 'Preface' by Wordsworth.

1802 *Lyrical Ballads* with revised 'Preface', 'Appendix' and additional poems; Wordsworth begins 'Immortality Ode' (stanzas 1–IV); writes 'Resolution and Independence'; visits France; marries Mary Hutchinson.

1803 Settlement agreed on debts owing to his father; first of six children born.

1804 Finishes 'Immortality Ode' (stanzas V–XI).

1805 Brother John drowned at sea; writes 'Elegiac Stanzas'.

1807 *Poems in Two Volumes*, including 'Elegiac Stanzas'.

1813 Appointed Distributor of Stamps for Westmoreland; moves to Rydal Mount.

1814 *The Excursion* published.

1815 *Poems in Two Volumes* published with new 'Preface' and 'Essay Supplementary'.
1843 Made Poet Laureate.
1850 Dies on 23 April.

Dates for *The Prelude*

Preface

We ought to impute the thoughts and attitudes
of the poem immediately to the dramatic
speaker, and if to the author at all, only by an
act of biographical inference.

W.K. Wimsatt and Monroe Beardsley

Another book about Wordsworth? Well, this isn't a book about
Wordsworth in the usual sense.

The Wordsworth of the conventional account is presented on the
assumption that his poetry is already *there* and all the critic can do is to
try to see it from a new point of view. Wordsworth's writing clearly interprets itself, like the proverbial sardine tin with the key for opening it
contained inside. Didn't Wordsworth himself explicitly and repeatedly
claim that his writing and his personal experience were the same thing
(and if not they should be)? Since his art and his life consist of the same
thing – an imaginative experience of Nature – the critic's job is to sift
through the words for the real Wordsworth hidden inside them. The
words are contradictory enough to make this quite an interesting job.

First of all there are the poems, several in different versions, and there
is the autobiographical poem, *The Prelude*, which exists in two main
versions (1805 and 1850) besides the two-part *Prelude* of 1799 and
other shorter passages in variant readings. To these have to be added
Wordsworth's prose works, including his 'Preface' to the *Lyrical Ballads*
and then his comments on his own work to contemporaries. All this is
immensely compounded when, seeking to join work and life, we add in
Wordsworth's friend and co-author, Coleridge, as well as his sister,
Dorothy, and her journal. Then there are the materials of Wordsworth's
biography and discussions of him by eminent contemporaries such as
Hazlitt and De Quincey. And so on. Assuming the obligation to reveal,

at the centre, a single, consistent self – a transcendent Wordsworth com-
prehending both lived biography and written poems – much conventional criticism recycles very much the same ideas. Wordsworth, like
the North Face of the Eiger, is just there, so all we can do is crawl up
him by slightly different routes.

The conventional presentation of Wordsworth rests on three related
assumptions:

1 William Wordsworth, the man, had a more or less direct experience
   of Nature.
2 Therefore his experience could pass more or less directly into his
   poetry (the work of his 'imagination').
3 Therefore someone reading the poetry now can have a more or less
   direct experience of what William Wordsworth experienced then,
   around the year 1800.

In the past decade or so a new paradigm has begun to take the field
of literary studies. This challenges the presuppositions of the previous
account, particularly by stressing that all we have now is not Wordsworth
himself but, at best, *traces* of Wordsworth in his writing:

1 Because adult human beings as 'speaking subjects' live and experience
   the world in and through language and since language is by nature
   shared and collective, there can be no more or less direct experience
   of Nature (or anything else, for that matter).
2 For the same reason, Wordsworth's 'experience' cannot pass more or
   less directly into art – his poetry is something different from his life.
3 For the same reason, again, Wordsworth's poems only come alive in
   the way we read them now – though we can only read at all by finding
   in them meanings different from those they may have had when they
   were first written down.

For brevity this summary has been somewhat schematic, and its
implications will, hopefully, become clearer in what follows. What it
does mean, however, is that I will try to keep the poet's life and the poems
separate very much as Wimsatt and Beardsley recommend in the
sentence put as an epigraph to this Preface. J. Hillis Miller in an article
on Wordsworth alludes to 'his writing, which is what is meant here by
"Wordsworth"'. And that is what 'Wordsworth' will mean here as well,
so that phrases like 'Wordsworth's intention' will refer to the effect of
the texts as we read them now. If I do refer to the historical author,
born 1770, died 80 years later, I shall try to speak of him as 'William
Wordsworth' (and this William Wordsworth hasn't been intending
anything since 1850).

Wordsworth now or then? How do we – today – make sense of these strange texts? For conventional criticism there is, in principle, no difficulty. William Wordsworth had some personal experiences, especially during the 1790s; he put them inside his poems, and so, if we use our imaginations, we can have more or less the same experiences reading the poems now.

There's something attractively comforting about this idea of a world without time, in which one can simply write 'Wordsworth says' believing that what he said in the 1790s is somehow the same as what he says now. Unfortunately, this is not the case. We are necessarily reading Wordsworth's texts in the present, in the 1990s, whether we admit it or not. From the signifier (shaped sound) we now produce what is signified (meaning).

Almost all the writing on Wordsworth is concerned with what the poems may have meant then, at some moment between 1790 and 1850. To make this assumption – that you can talk about what Wordsworth meant then – you have to rely now, in the present, on a historical narrative, which construes Wordsworth's past moment – 1792, 1805, 1815 or whenever – as a then in relation to other thens. Wordsworth's writing is itself powerful testimony to this effect. In *The Prelude* Wordsworth was anxious to elaborate a historical narrative of the then of 1789–97 though he could only do so from within his sense of the now of 1805, as we can now see pretty clearly. There is no escape from this dialectic, which means that we can only define a historical Wordsworth in terms of a narrative we uphold now. It is important to relate Wordsworth to his historical moment but it is even more important to look at the ground we are standing on now. Giving attention to the then should not be allowed to obscure the now and the simple question of what these texts can mean in the 1990s. Pleasure and the question of ideology both return discussion to the present. Pleasure manifestly can only be pleasure we feel now, dependent upon the fantasies – conscious and unconscious – the texts make available to present readers. As for ideology, it is not just an object which we come to see within the perspective of a historical narrative – it is also a form of lived experience. In terms of ideology, as I shall hope to show, there are strong continuities flowing between the Wordsworth of the 1790s and the circumstances in which he is still read.

If Wordsworth's poetry were *really* unique, the Great Individual expressing himself only on his own terms (as conventional criticism says), it's hard to know how other people could read it. Since this is not the case, Wordsworth's work has to be viewed for the ways it's like that of other people – typical, representative, intertextual. And it is typical in that it partakes of ideological structures of the 1790s that we still inhabit today.

Obviously a central reason Wordsworth is read today is that he remains solidly part of the literary canon, taught in schools and universities. But Wordsworth works not just because the syllabus imposes him on us but also because we can find something there that answers us. I am interested in what makes it possible for us to read Wordsworth, and so in the conditions of possibility generating his work, the ideologies it reproduces, the patterning of ideas, tropes and fantasies which we share – or must learn to share – otherwise we couldn't make any sense of the poems. I'd like to know how it works for us (if it does). For we are reading Wordsworth as our contemporary whether we admit it or not.

So I am not going to try to give a new 'interpretation' of Wordsworth and say something different from everybody else. Rather, I shall draw on and draw together other writing on Wordsworth from within the new paradigm partly because I want to show there is indeed a degree of consensus there. And for the same reason I shall keep theory off-stage trusting that much of the new paradigm is sufficiently agreed to remain implicit. All my references are in the Notes section at the end of the book, which the reader does not have to read or refer to unless she or he wishes. I shall make no attempt to discuss every poem and will concentrate unashamedly on Wordsworth before 1810 – the main poems and especially *The Prelude* – because that's what everyone else does.

Facing Wordsworth now and then is a way to live into the dead writing so it may partly come alive for us. I first came across Wordsworth at school when I was 17. Looking back now I remember (or think I remember) being unable to resist what Marjorie Levinson calls his 'seductive instruction'. I was stirred, felt there was something going on but that there were two blank obstacles to enjoying the poetry. One was the abstract, generalized, diffuse language –

> And I have felt
> A presence that disturbs me with the joy
> Of elevated thoughts: a sense sublime
> Of something far more deeply interfused . . .

– that sort of thing, vaguely transcendental despite the recognizable anecdotes about birdsnesting and skating. The other problem I recall was that I couldn't understand anyone taking Nature so seriously. Everyone enjoys walking in the country and fresh air but for Wordsworth these ordinary things seemed to be wildly overblown and humourlessly exaggerated beyond all reach of common sense. I can now see I was treating the poems as though what mattered was how well they referred to Nature, and in this I was not alone.

Seeing Wordsworth in terms of now and then may hold his writing in a tension, an important tension. On one side we are pulled by awareness that his language is stylized, dated, very obviously constructed and artificial, as is his reproduction of structures of ideology (Nature and Imagination). Both are markedly an aspect of the Wordsworth then, belonging to his time, certainly, but they are also part of a textuality that can be shown to persist into our now and something more like an immediate apprehension of Wordsworth now. So the question – what Wordsworth means by Nature and how far we can go along with it – will be my starting point in the first chapter.

No work is unique or individual and I would like to thank a number of people who took time and trouble to comment on my manuscript: Kate Belsey, Stewart Crehan, Keith Hanley, Kate McGowan, Steve Rigby. I also learned a great deal from talking about Wordsworth with Rob Lapsley. Of course what goes into a book is one thing and what comes out for other people is another.

I would also like to acknowledge the following permissions to reproduce copyright work: Canongate Press for the poem 'A Highland Woman' from the volume *Spring Tide and Neap Tide* by Sorley Maclean; Warner Chappell Music Ltd/International Music Publications for some words from 'Like a Prayer' (Madonna Ciccone, Patrick Leonard), reproduced by permission © 1989.

1

Nature and Imagination

There's no more nature
Samuel Beckett
Endgame

Wordsworth is not interested in Nature. Anyone seriously interested in Nature would do far better to read, say, Erasmus Darwin's beautiful and detailed scientific cataloguing of the differentiated realities and specificities of the natural world in his poem *The Botanic Garden* (1791) than a single line of Wordsworth. For even Wordsworth's best descriptions of the natural world are hopelessly vague and undefined – clouds whirl across the sky, the moon shines, daffodils bounce about in high winds.

However, it is often wrongly thought that among poets Wordsworth is the one especially interested in Nature. Nature in this sense means something rather different from the natural world. To be 'interested in Nature' in this way means rather, as it was suggested in the Preface, that William Wordsworth experienced the beauty of the natural world and that his poetry makes a similar experience possible for the reader. This is a view I intend to contest at every turn, though it is one still so widely believed that I shall deliberately take the risk of labouring the question in this chapter.

The first thing to be said is that poetry is not and cannot be itself an experience of Nature but, at best, the *representation* of an experience of Nature in poetic form. Wordsworth's poetry frequently seeks to represent someone having a direct and unmediated experience of the real. In this respect his poetry supports the view that perceptions pass from out there more or less transparently into the inner self. This view is mistaken, as an example will hope to demonstrate.

'There was a Boy'

A paragraph in *The Prelude* (originally published separately in the *Lyrical Ballads*) describes a boy from Windermere calling to the owls. It appears in both the 1805 and 1850 versions referring to a third person, though in a manuscript (MS. JJ) it is phrased in terms of 'I'. Coleridge in his usual hysterical style said of the concluding lines of the passage that even if he had come across them 'running wild in the deserts of Arabia' he would instantly have cried out '"Wordsworth!"'. In the 1850 version of *The Prelude* (the one I shall use throughout) the lines begin as follows:

> There was a Boy: ye knew him well, ye cliffs
> And islands of Winander! – many a time
> At evening, when the earliest stars began
> To move along the edges of the hills,
> Rising or setting, would he stand alone
> Beneath the trees or by the glimmering lake,
> And there, with fingers interwoven, both hands
> Pressed closely palm to palm, and to his mouth
> Uplifted, he, as through an instrument,
> Blew mimic hootings to the silent owls,
> That they might answer him; and they would shout
> Across the watery vale, and shout again,
> Responsive to his call, with quivering peals,
> And long halloos and screams, and echoes wild
> Of jocund din; and, when a lengthened pause
> Of silence came and baffled his best skill,
> Then sometimes, in that silence while he hung
> Listening . . .
>
> *(1850 version, Book V: 364–82)*

I'm going to stop the poem at this point and imagine different ways it could have gone on.

What we have so far is a fairly ordinary boyish activity for someone brought up in the country (though I doubt whether you really can mimic owls this way). By a lake between some hills a boy makes owl-noises by blowing through his hands; the owls mistake these for another owl and hoot back, the noise echoing round the scene; but at a certain point the owls stop and refuse to call back, though in the silence the boy goes on straining to hear them.

So much for the event and his perceptions. How might those *perceptions* be interpreted and *experienced*? A traditional reading would of course take up the perception in a Christian framework:

> 1 Then sometimes, in that silence while he hung
>   Listening, after such cries, beyond the world,

He heard a still small Voice reminding him
Of Love which moves the sun and other stars.

The moment of silence is experienced as the ineffable Word of God, as something positive and present. So it might be also according to the more recent religion of love, which took over many of its features from Christianity:

2   Then sometimes, in that silence while he hung
    Listening, he thought he saw her lovely form
    Reflected in the lake, while far away
    The hills and sky were whispering her name.

The silence and beauty of the scene is felt to affirm the moment of romance, that the sexual relation is possible.

Today we might expect the landscape to be experienced in a more negative way, particularly following the Modernist tradition (which frequently assumes some transcendental meaning behind reality and then registers its absence). In a Modernist poem, such as Eliot's 'The Waste Land', the silence could well be imagined in relation to 'the universe' and its supposed 'indifference' to human purposes:

3   Then sometimes, in that silence while he hung
    Listening and thinking there, he found he could
    Not speak and his eyes failed, he was neither
    Living nor dead, and he knew nothing,
    Looking in the heart of light, the silence.
    Waste and empty the mere.

This is a rendering in terms of a negative theology (God is dead). Similarly, and on the precedent of the Marabar caves incident in Forster's *A Passage to India*, the owls' halloos and screams and echoes might seem a token of the void Mrs Moore in Chapter 14 of that novel feels is at the centre of human experience:

4   Then sometimes, in that silence while he hung
    Listening to overlapping howls, he felt
    The lack of all distinction in that sound
    Whose echoes seemed to say 'bou-oum', 'ou-boum',
    And, motionless with sudden horror, knew
    'Let there be Light' meant nothing more than 'boum'.

In Sartre's 1938 novel, *Nausea*, the hero, Roquentin, finds himself faced with certain objects – a air of braces, a piece of paper in the street, the root of a chestnut tree – but is unable to define them except in human categories and these, he feels, are inadequate. At such moments he has a sense of nausea, and there is no reason why he should not respond to the objects in a Wordsworthian landscape the same way:

> 5 Then sometimes, in that silence while he hung
>   Listening, the empty scene pressed on his mind
>   As something quite beyond all human thought
>   Existing there so fully *in itself*
>   It made him feel himself to be *de trop*,
>   Unnecessary, nauseous and absurd.

A Sartrian interpretation of the boy's perceptions would stress a sense of distance between the human and the natural rather than their potential correspondence. Rejecting the Romantic wish for a union between Nature and Imagination, a strand in twentieth-century thought has tried to realize a sense of the absolute otherness of being and the real, what is *there* prior to any human imposition of meaning on it.

It is in this spirit that Wittgenstein writes in 1921, 'It is not how things are in the world that is mystical, but that it exists'; or again that in 1935 Heidegger opens his book, *An Introduction to Metaphysics*, with the question, 'Why are there essents [things that are] rather than nothing? The poetry of Wallace Stevens, though concerned with the natural world only to demonstrate how far the Imagination exceeds it, frequently aims to render a sense of the otherness of the real, for example in 'The Snow Man'. A similar manoeuvre could work on this scene:

> 6 Then sometimes, in that silence while he hung
>   Listening, he found it hard not to believe
>   The peaceful scene would enter unawares
>   Into his peaceful mind, and see instead
>   Nothing that was not there and the nothing
>   That was.

Some of the earlier poetry of Charles Tomlinson also contrives to give a sense of the otherness of the real, when, for example, 'Hawks' in *Written on Water* (1972) moves away from banal ideological notions of the fierceness of hawks to a scientifically based recognition of their existence as a species ('The pair / After their kind are lovers . . .').

Some of my versions are less plausible than others, yet it would not be difficult to go on spinning them out – a Darwinian/Tennysonian response to the owls as ferocious predators going off to tear at helpless field-mice so the speaker experiences Nature as red in tooth and claw or an ecological interpretation of the owls as admirably and self-sufficiently uninterested in the exploitative attempt of the boy to impose human values on their harmoniously balanced interaction within the eco-system (never eating too many field-mice, for instance). My limping blank-verse examples are meant to substantiate the view that perceptions of the real do not pass unmediated into the self and so do not determine how those perceptions are *experienced*. A perception always has to be interpreted and can be interpreted in many ways. Or, to put it in Wordsworth's terms, Nature depends upon the human Imagination.

After these parodies we may turn to the version William Wordsworth had settled on by the time of his death in 1850:

> Then sometimes, in that silence while he hung
> Listening, a gentle shock of mild surprise
> Has carried far into his heart the voice
> Of mountain torrents; or the visible scene
> Would enter unawares into his mind,
> With all its solemn imagery, its rocks,
> Its woods, and that uncertain heaven, received
> Into the bosom of the steady lake.
>
> (V: 381–8)

The invented versions show in sharp relief what assumptions the Wordsworth passage enacts. It envisages that, entering 'unawares', perceptions pass more or less directly into the mind and can be experienced for what they are, so demonstrating that a beautiful landscape and inner experience match each other.

'There was a Boy' works hard to try to make everything conduct to a single end: an affirmation of the reciprocal relationship (or correspondence or bond) between natural world and the inner self. The entry of the impression of the objects, far from being alien or threatening, is welcomed as beneficent – the 'visible scene' is 'solemn', perhaps 'uncertain', but it is sanctioned – and – sanctified – as a form of 'heaven'. Objective world and subjective experience are desirably unified, the otherness of nature being overcome and made good through its incorporation into the self. Affirmation, however, depends upon its opposite, denial and the fear that goes with that (you don't assert what can never be disputed). Since correspondence or unity is *desired* and since desire originates in lack (is defined by its endeavour to overcome lack), the passage covertly admits what it denies so warmly – non-correspondence, the absence of unity, separation between subject and object.

Affirmation of unity is reiterated across several levels (it is overdetermined). At the level of narrated event the owls call to each other but they and the boy also mimic each other and in turn are echoed by the hills. At the level of vocabulary, the external perceptions are *already* shaped in consonance with their inward destination, anthropomorphized, so that, for example, the objective sound of the mountain torrents, without forcing, has been made personal by being termed a 'voice' and the sky lent a spiritual connotation as an 'uncertain heaven'. In a complex effect which W. K. Wimsatt explains as 'romantic wit', aspects of what is objectively perceived are repeated and reappear in the subjective mode of metaphor. Sky is reflected in the water but this external feature is mobilized as a trope for the way the landscape enters the boy. Anticipating that the 'imagery' will be 'received' into his *mind* or 'bosom' we find in fact that it is received into the *lake*. De Quincey, in an acute piece of critical analysis, sees exactly the main impact of this passage when he says of it:

> This very expression, 'far,' by which space and its infinities are attributed to the human heart, and to its capacities of re-echoing the sublimities of nature, has always struck me as with a flash of sublime revelation.

External scenery works to mirror and even provide terms for the expression of subjectivity. To the extent it is possible, subject and object are to be brought together, brought together because they are actually separate.

But why? What desire may be at stake in wishing for such a union? As more than one critic has noticed, when the passage appears in *The Prelude* (V: 364ff.) the boy dies before he was twelve, suggesting that some kind of transgression has to be paid for. From among a number of motives one in particular could be picked out. The boy tries to lure Nature as the other (he calls to the owls to treat him as one of them) and in turn, 'unawares' (so it's said) is won over by the other. Nature 'would enter' him on the model of the way the sky is 'received' passively into the 'bosom' of the lake. This passage on the boy seems to bury the desire to seduce the other beneath the desire to be seduced by it (and it would be hard to mistake the gender and parental identity of the imagined other). The boy of Winander passage provides an opportunity too good to miss for broaching such questions though they will need to be taken up again in more detail later on.

Being and meaning

Empiricism can be defined as the assumption that human beings achieve knowledge more or less directly from experience, and it forms the main English tradition in epistemology. This narrative of the boy of Winander does not count as a philosophic statement though it represents in poetic form a view or attitude consistent with empiricism: that the landscape is rawly and nakedly *there* and so can be assimilated as part of the boy's experience. In this respect the passage typifies Wordsworth's belief that the being of the natural world and humanly constructed meaning can be brought together in a unified presence. My assumption, shared widely enough, is that being and meaning exclude each other.

There is no question here of post-structuralists who don't know the difference between a window on the sixth floor and a door on the ground floor, no question, that is, of denying the reality of the real. The real exists and we live in it, or as Hamm says in Beckett's play, *Endgame*, 'you're on earth, there's no cure for that!'. But the real as being exists outside signification, in fact resists signification and the order of meaning (there are no holes in the real). As speaking subjects, people live not only in the real but also in the world of signs, and so have access to the real only in so far as it has been made to signify, in so far as its traces have already been made over into humanly constructed meaning. There are a number of ways to give brief support for this position.

One would be to appeal to recent developments in cognitive psychology, which illustrate how much perception depends upon knowledge rather than vice versa. A traditional assumption about seeing the world would be that a retinal image copies reality and the brain copies a retinal image, much as (in the Quattrocento painting convention) a realist painting or photograph is thought to copy the real. In fact, to see an object 'generally involves knowledge of the object derived from previous experience'. So R. L. Gregory says, and demonstrates with the now well-known example (among many others) of how lines of the same length are perceived as longer or shorter depending on whether we think of them as corners projecting towards or receding from us.

Or we could consider the human infant, so-called from the Latin *infans*, not speaking. A newborn baby wholly inhabits the world of being and is at one with its own body, and so with everything. Yet gradually a margin opens at the limits of its being, a gap or fissure it seeks to fill with meaning and the seeming plentitude of signs. To become a speaking subject within discourse, to enter meaning, is to lose the object in the real and endlessly re-seek it as an object to be found in and through language: 'the symbol manifests itself first of all as the murder of the thing'. Hence, everything for human beings – after infancy – is caught up to a greater or lesser extent in a field of desire and cannot be felt as existing in itself.

A further instance would be the social construction of reality. Marx argues that a perception which might seem to be physiologically compact, merely a matter of the body, is in fact taken up differently in different cultures shaped by different modes of production: 'Hunger is hunger, but the hunger gratified by cooked meat eaten with a knife and fork is a different hunger from that which bolts down raw meat with the aid of hand, nail and tooth.' Following this line of thought the Marxist writer, Christopher Caudwell, claims that human production in its development across history has always transformed the natural world for human purposes. Appropriately enough, the point is made with reference to Wordsworth: 'Wordsworth's "Nature" is of course a Nature freed of wild beasts and danger by aeons of human work, a Nature in which the poet, enjoying a comfortable income, lives on the products of industrialism even while he enjoys the natural scene "unspoilt" by industrialism.'

Cognitive psychology, psychoanalysis, historical materialism – each can be adduced to testify that for us experience of the real is always already constructed. A more germane example for poetry and Wordsworth can be found in the history of metaphor. From the time of classical rhetoric personification is the name given to a trope or figure of speech in which something non-human – an inanimate object, an animal or an abstract quality – is given human attributes ('a raging sea' for example, or 'time flies'), a procedure which John Ruskin in 1856 named 'pathetic fallacy'. In a long history, shared codes of personification were presided over by socially instituted myths but, as will be suggested further on, Romanticism with Wordsworth shifted personification away from a collective to a (would-be) personal dimension.

Following on from the work of Heidegger and Sartre (as was mentioned in relation to my versions 5 and 6 of 'There was a Boy'), the French novelist Alain Robbe-Grillet in the 1950s argued against what he termed 'humanism', that is, an anthropomorphism which asserts 'solidarity between the human spirit and the world'. Rejecting this 'metaphysical pact', Robbe-Grillet favours acceptance that 'things are things, and man is only man [sic]'. And he shows anthropomorphist humanism at work in metaphor. Even a casual reference to 'a village "crouching" in the hollow of a valley' assumes that human feelings find their natural correspondence in the world while to say the village was 'situated' in the hollow of the valley would not. Saying 'No' to this humanism Robbe-Grillet determined that he would 'record the separation between an object and myself'.

Now this is stirringly anti-Romantic and anti-Wordsworthian, for obviously Wordsworth's project is to record a sense of the unity between an object and himself. Yet things turned out to be not so neat as Robbe-Grillet hoped. His manifesto commitment to writing about the real on its own or at least in non-anthropomorphic terms runs into several difficulties. One is that passages which attempt to describe the real 'as it is' actually foreground their origin in human discourse; prolonged 'objective' description rapidly turns into a kind of *paysage intérieur* and form of fantasy. But the strongest objection is that you can't sustain a binary opposition between a metaphorical discourse and one that is clinically literal (Robbe-Grillet actually espoused that of science). Metaphor is integral to human language, dormant but still alive in even the most seemingly denotative references to 'the hand of a clock', 'the leg of a chair' or even to something being 'in front of' something else (in some languages you can't say this). The village 'crouching' in the hollow is inescapable, and so are things like Wordsworth's allusion to the sky as 'heaven' and to 'the voice' of mountain torrents. If we are always anthropomorphizing, if human subjects have *no alternative* but to refer to what is beyond them on their own terms, then Wordsworth's attempt to celebrate the way the real shapes human experience comes unstuck once again.

Philip Sidney states that 'the poet . . . nothing affirms, and therefore never lieth'. Wordsworth writes as a poet, not as a philosopher, and there is no question here of trying to *refute* him. But to argue that being and meaning do not coincide is a necessary means of refusing to submit to the views and attitudes so much at home in Wordsworth's poetry, and, even now, in the main body of his critics. If we start from the position that the real is constructed we have every reason to examine how Wordsworth's poetry contrives to give the *effect of the real*.

In a sentence cited above Christopher Caudwell indicates that Wordsworth's Nature is produced in the process of human history and through human labour, that it is in fact ideological. To begin an exploration of this aspect of Wordsworth's poetry (while weaving into the text further confirmation that landscape is not just perceived but interpreted) I shall contrast two descriptions written in the eighteenth century within 85 years of each other.

Windsor Forest in Pope and 'Tintern Abbey' in Wordsworth

Alexander Pope's *Windsor Forest* (1713) opens with a sweeping, exuberant and somewhat shocking insistence that England, as represented by Windsor Forest, is the Garden of Eden:

> The Groves of *Eden*, vanish'd now so long,
> Live in Description, and look green in Song:
> *These*, were my Breast inspired with equal Flame,
> Like them in Beauty, should be like in Fame.
> Here Hills and Vales, the Woodland and the Plain,
> Here Earth and Water seem to strive again,

Not *Chaos*-like together crush'd and bruis'd,
But as the World, harmoniously confus'd:
Where Order in Variety we see,
And where, tho' all things differ, all agree.
Here waving Groves a checquer'd Scene display,
And part admit and part exclude the Day;
As some coy Nymph her Lover's warm Address
Nor quite indulges, nor can quite repress.
There, interspers'd in Lawns and opening Glades,
Thin trees arise that shun each others Shades.
Here in full Light the russet Plains extend;
There wrapt in Clouds the blueish Hills ascend:
Ev'n the wild Heath displays her Purple Dies,
And 'midst the Desart fruitful Fields arise,
That crown'd with tufted Trees and springing corn,
Like verdant Isles the sable Waste adorn.
Let *India* boast her Plants, nor envy we
The weeping Amber or the balmy Tree,
While by our Oaks the precious Loads are born,
And realms commanded which those Trees adorn.
Not proud *Olympus* yields a nobler Sight,
Tho' Gods assembled grace his tow'ring Height,
Than what more humble Mountains offer here,
Where, in their Blessings, all those Gods appear.
See Pan with Flocks, with Fruits *Pomona* crown'd,
Here blushing *Flora* paints th'enamel'd Ground,
Here *Ceres'* Gifts in waving Prospect stand,
And nodding tempt the joyful Reaper's Hand,
Rich Industry sits smiling on the Plains,
And Peace and Plenty tell, a STUART reigns.

Wordsworth's 'Lines, Composed a few miles above Tintern Abbey' (13 July 1798) begins very differently:

FIVE years have past; five summers, with the length
Of five long winters! and again I hear
These waters, rolling from their mountain-springs
With a soft inland murmur. – Once again
Do I behold these steep and lofty cliffs,
That on a wild secluded scene impress
Thoughts of more deep seclusion; and connect
The landscape with the quiet of the sky.
The day is come when I again repose
Here, under this dark sycamore, and view
These plots of cottage-ground, these orchard-tufts,
Which at this season, with their unripe fruits,

Are clad in one green hue, and lose themselves
'Mid groves and copses. Once again I see
These hedge-rows, hardly hedge-rows, little lines
Of sportive wood run wild: these pastoral farms,
Green to the very door; and wreaths of smoke
Sent up, in silence, from among the trees!
With some uncertain notice, as might seem
Of vagrant dwellers in the houseless woods,
Or of some Hermit's cave, where by his fire
The Hermit sits alone.

Now these are named as different parts of England, Windsor Forest
in Berkshire and Tintern Abbey on the River Wye between Gwent and
Gloucestershire. But as landscapes, as concretizations of the natural
world, perceived in the everyday, they hardly differ and might even be
the same place. Both consist of patches of open landscape with trees
(both writers specify 'groves' and 'tufts'), both have farms surrounded
by areas not cultivated; in both a flat plain in the foreground gives
way to hills in the background and in both there are streams with running
'water'. Although each writer's eye picks out different details (one names
'Oaks', the other a 'sycamore'), in default of the titles it would be impossible to tell exactly where each landscape was except that it certainly
wasn't Provence or Tuscany or the Black Forest – generalized North
European, probably English but not unmistakably so.

Yet Pope and Wordsworth each interpret the 'same' natural scene
very differently. For Pope it is typical, construed within a shared literary
convention (the pastoral) stretching back via the classical poets of
Greece and Rome to the book of Genesis. His is a Newtonian landscape
whose explicable rationality contains difference within an overriding
order ('Not *Chaos*-like'), even in the detail by which the height of the
trees spontaneously matches their distance apart ('Thin Trees arise
that shun each others Shades') just as the red of the plain forms an
aesthetic harmony with the blue of the hills. The natural world is valued
insofar as it submits to human control – 'Even the wild heath' is useful
as a source of dyeing material – and that control is both avowedly social
and historically specific. What is lacking in this paradise can be imported
from an India now under the aegis of British imperialism ('by our Oaks
the precious Loads are born'), while the general increase in agricultural
production of this re-found Eden is guaranteed by the post-1688 con-
stitutional settlement – 'Peace and Plenty tell, a STUART reigns'. When
description of scenery gives way to a person – a point of identification
for the reader – that person is a monarch and at the centre of the
social web.

For Wordsworth the landscape comes as a direct personal experience – it is to be his landscape perceived by his specifically situated eye ('under this dark sycamore') and recalled from his memory of it. A discourse of personal pronouns ('I' four times), demonstratives ('These', 'Here') and the use throughout of the present tense give the effect of an individual in the process of thinking and feeling – the hedge-rows (in a double take) are looked at again and reinterpreted as 'hardly hedge-rows, little lines / Of sportive wood run wild'. The self represented is apparently beyond or outside the social formation. In symbolic consistency with this, the natural world is valued in so far as it seems to escape human control – for Pope 'the wild heath' matters if it can be used whereas Wordsworth relishes the way cultivated hedge-rows, in returning to wood, seem to 'run wild'. There is no overt equivalent for Wordsworth of Pope's (wholly traditional) eroticization of landscape (with its 'coy nymph' and tempted reaper). And of course while Pope's interpretation of the landscape culminates in the sovereignty of Queen Anne, Wordsworth's comes to rest in the imagined figure (actually out of sight) of the solitary individual in retreat from society, the Hermit sitting alone, his surrogate within the represented scene, and ours as readers.

In each case a similar set of perceptions is interpreted in a way which is historical, that is, ideological: Pope's landscape is construed according to the rational values of his society, Wordsworth's according to the Romanticism of his. There are, however, respects in which the landscape in both writers is constructed in the same way and on the same terms. Though there is agricultural production in both landscapes, in neither is anyone working or sweating (Pope's 'joyful reaper' is not reaping but being tempted). Both, then, are contemplated scenes. Although *Windsor Forest* does not make an issue of its speaker, there is a viewer for this perspective nevertheless, someone who gestures towards the external facts of the plains which are 'Here' and the hills which are 'There' with a confidence approaching that with which the 'I' of 'Tintern Abbey' refers to being 'Here' under the sycamore and seeing 'these' cliffs. Pope's speaker perceives very much what any educated gentlemen might have been thought to see in 1713 while the I of the 'Tintern Abbey' passage is securely posed outside obvious social designation, yet both extracts share a sense of the every world as perceived by an individual. Nevertheless, the contrast shows that very much the same landscape *qua* landscape is very different for Pope and for Wordsworth.

Wordsworth's development

The question of whether (how far?) the real determines our interpretation of it or we determine our interpretation of it – the epistemological question – lies at the heart of much conventional Wordsworth criticism. For this makes its home in a prolonged and intricate discussion of Wordsworth's development, taking its cue from the kind of statement explicitly repeated in Wordsworth's poetry: that the Wordsworthian subject moves from seeing Nature as good and doing things for him towards awareness that he is independent of Nature and must rely on his own resources to find these good experiences with Nature, from dependence on Nature to affirmation of the power of the Imagination. Conventional criticism exercises itself at great length over what Nature really gives to a passive Wordsworth in terms of perception and what an active Wordsworth really imagines in excess of any perception.

We don't have to go down this road, and the question of whether Nature gives or the subject imagines is really a noose you don't have to put your head into. For it only becomes valid on the basis of an assumption that Nature (perception) *could* give something (interpretation of that perception) and so the view that Nature gives can be contrasted with one in which the imagination is considered more or less autonomous. My hope is that the argument so far has got us over that. If it has, if we may simply step past the possibility that the real in itself may be nice or nasty, kind and loving or something else, then the way is open to proceed quietly on the assumption that Nature exists as we appropriate it and that for human beings the real appears only in our representations of it. We can forget about perception and the real, and think rather about the phenomenology of the two positions, what the difference between these two experiences may mean.

The broad outline of what Wordsworth's explicit views are is not really in dispute. Position 1 (dependence on Nature), exemplified earlier in the description of the boy of Winander, is well set out in the fourth paragraph of the 'Tintern Abbey' poem:

> For nature then
> (The coarser pleasures of my boyish days,
> And their glad animal movements all gone by)
> To me was all in all. – I cannot paint
> What then I was. The sounding cataract
> Haunted me like a passion: the tall rock,
> The mountain, and the deep and gloomy wood,
> Their colours and their forms, were then to me
> An appetite; a feeling and a love,

> That had no need of a remoter charm,
> By thought supplied, nor any interest
> Unborrowed from the eye.

The mountain and the wood *are* an appetite and the experience, supposedly, follows directly from the perception, the 'feeling' from 'the eye'.
So it is again in a passage from *The Recluse*, which was written and
published separately:

> my voice proclaims
> How exquisitely the individual Mind
> (And the progressive powers perhaps no less
> Of the whole species) to the external World
> Is fitted: – and how exquisitely, too –
> Theme this but little heard of among men –
> The external World is fitted to the Mind . . .
> (*Part I, Book I: 826–32*)

(In his copy of Wordsworth, William Blake, who believed that consciousness constructs the reality it experiences, wrote, 'You shall not
bring me down to believe such fitting & fitted. I know better and please
your Lordship'.)

Position 2 (autonomy of human imagination) is affirmed later in the
'Tintern Abbey' poem:

> For I have learned
> To look on nature, not as in the hour
> Of thoughtless youth; but hearing oftentimes
> The still, sad music of humanity . . .

and in stanza X of the 'Immortality' ode:

> We will grieve not, rather find
> Strength in what remains behind;
> In the primal sympathy
> Which having been must ever be;
> In the soothing thoughts that spring
> Out of human suffering . . .

Position 2 is said to be a recompense, but only a partial recompense, for
the loss of Position 1.

As anticipated in the first four stanzas of the 'Immortality' ode (drafted
in 1802), from 1804 Wordsworth's poetry increasingly acknowledges a
human recognition of loss and separateness, as for example in 'Elegiac
Stanzas, Suggested by a picture of Peele Castle, in a story, painted by Sir
George Beaumont'. Recalling a time when he saw the castle over a period
of weeks, not in a storm but in sunny, windless calm, Wordsworth feels

enthralled by a sense of dyadic unity between castle and sea, the human artifact reflected in its natural surroundings (as so often, the castle symbolizes the fortress of the self):

> So pure the sky, so quiet was the air!
> So like, so very like, was day to day!
> When'er I looked, thy Image still was there;
> It trembled, but it never passed away.

Taking this memory, he says how he would have represented it in art:

> Ah! then, if mine had been the Painter's hand,
> To express what then I saw; and add the gleam,
> The light that never was, on sea or land,
> The consecration, and the Poet's dream;
>
> I would have planted thee, thou hoary Pile
> Amid a world how different from this!
> Beside a sea that could not cease to smile;
> On tranquil land, beneath a sky of bliss.

Now the former vision of unity is rejected:

> So once it would have been, – 'tis so no more;
> I have submitted to a new control:
> A power is gone, which nothing can restore;
> A deep distress hath humanised my Soul.

The passing from the moment of vision to becoming humanized is acknowledged as a 'loss', one which leads him now to prefer the picture of the castle in a storm:

> And this huge Castle, standing here sublime,
> I love to see the look with which it braves,
> Cased in the unfeeling armour of old time,
> The lightning, the fierce wind, and trampling waves.

Like the castle, the self is desired as free-standing and self-defining.

Clearly enough, this poem contrasts a former state in which the self, like the castle, merges into and seems 'at one' with the natural world, and another state in which the castle of the ego stands alone by defending itself against the natural world. And, clearly enough, attending merely to what the poem says ignores the tricky questions that open up when we ask how it says it. Isn't the rugged castle to some degree at one with the wild storm beating against it since they fit together in the same Romantic scene (an idea in accord rather with Position 1)? And surely the vision of the castle reflected in the calm ocean is in part acknowledged as a human construction since it is thought of as a pictorial representation (in accord with Position 2)? Even so, the broad distinction between the two positions holds.

If, as I think we must, we move past the unanswerable question of what the real might be like in itself, then we face the more interesting and answerable question of what it means in Wordsworth for the subject to think of Nature as good for it and then move on to think of itself as autonomous. There are different ways of phrasing the answer. In Ovid's *Metamorphoses* (iii: 318–510) Narcissus falls in love with his own reflection in the water of a spring, his likeness as it depends on the Other. At first he loves it believing it to be someone else but comes to recognize that it is an image of himself ('*iste ego sum*', line 463) so that he has a degree of autonomy from the Other. Borrowing from Sophocles, Freud tells a story of how the little boy at first seeks only the mother, has to give her up, but in doing so may come to identify with the father and his place in (patriarchal) society. Lacan writes of a transition from demand to desire. The infant directs its demand for love to the Other in the assumption that the Other can satisfy its needs (nature seeming to be 'all in all'); entering language the child finds its demand for love has to be put in terms which are shared by everyone; humanized by its loss, it desires an object which is always moving away from it, like the wave from the bow of a ship.

Whatever the terms in which it is defined, the movement from nature into culture, from seeming dependence on the natural Other to seeming independence within the human or social Other, Wordsworth's poetry certainly explains and dramatizes that development. However, if, as has been proposed here, we withdraw from the view that the 'same' individual lives the life recorded in the biographies and in the poetry, and if, further, we bracket (as we have to) this whole question of a possible relation to the real, then the development issue reveals itself as much less absorbing. Frankly, robbed of its epistemological pretensions, it turns out to be a rather banal matter of growing up.

With the question of the real firmly shelved, other questions come onto the agenda, particularly as these concern text, representation and how Wordsworth's poetry produces meanings. Writing as a card-carrying empiricist (and, so, typically English) A.H. Clough in 1869 commented on Wordsworth's poetry:

> What is meant when people complain of him as mawkish, is a different matter. It is, I believe, that instead of looking directly at an object, and considering it as a thing in itself, he takes the sentiment produced by it in his own mind, as the thing, as the important and really real fact. The real things cease to be real; the world no longer exists; all that exists is the feeling, somehow generated in the poetry's sensibility.

Clough is surely right. Wordsworth's poetry is concerned not with 'real things' but with 'the feeling' and the representation of a psychological effect.

Being and meaning do not coincide: although this is the position from which the present book is written, no one has to accept it as necessarily true. From it does ensue a critical distance on the poetry, which should make analysis easier. By not being sucked into sympathetic identification with Wordsworth's 'vision' (Nature and Imagination) as the very asking price for entry to discussion of this writing we may be able to appreciate better how it works. For example, to assert *contra* Wordsworth that meaning is exterior to being, immediately throws a powerful interrogatory light on the question: why does Wordsworth so passionately and consistently demand that being should yield itself so readily to meaning, that the external be made internal, that object be held in a relation of union with subjectivity? Why is the typical movement of his verse, predicated on awareness of the difference between subject and object, into attempted elision of that difference?

For an answer to this I shall turn first of all in the next chapter to a social and historical analysis of the Romantic situation and Wordsworth's response to it in *The Prelude*. Then in subsequent chapters I will aim to unpack the sense of unity between subject and object not by submitting it to ideological critique from the 'outside' but rather by considering what – on its own terms – it is trying, and failing, to do.

2

Romantic Ideology

Between 1793 and 1798 Wordsworth lost the
world merely to gain his immortal soul.

Jerome McGann

It is a commonplace of literary criticism to define Romanticism by its
quest for the reconciliation of subject and object. 'The common feat of
the romantic nature poets was to read meanings into landscape', writes
W.K. Wimsatt in 1949, and in 1953 M.H. Abrams in his magisterial
book, *The Mirror and the Lamp*, makes the same point like this:

> What is distinctive in the poetry of Wordsworth and Coleridge is not the
> attribution of a life and soul to nature, but the repeated formulation of
> this outer life as a contribution of, or else as in constant reciprocation
> with, the life and soul of man the observer.

Two years later, the very distinguished European critic, René Wellek,
could look back over several generations of critical work analysing the
Romantic project and refer confidently to the 'essence and nature' of
European and English Romanticism as 'that attempt, apparently doorned
to failure and abandoned by our time, to identify subject and object,
to reconcile man and nature, consciousness and unconsciousness by
poetry which is "the first and last of all knowledge"'.

This demand for unity between subject and object cannot be understood apart from the sense of individual identity it may express. Since
the Renaissance (whenever exactly that is considered to have begun),
European culture has increasingly circumscribed a separated identity
for the individual; towards the end of the eighteenth century, this
process began to open up a radically new sense of the self as enjoying
an inward and personal potentiality. There are two possible historical
assessments of this new sense of private identity. One position would
be that to find the significance of human life not in the traditional

transcendental sanctions of a supernatural Christianity but rather in the historical development of a significant relation between spirit and materiality, subjective consciousness and objective reality, culminating in the augmented self-consciousness of Romanticism, was, for all the difficulties, an unambiguous sign of human progress (of this view Hegel is the most powerful and sophisticated proponent). An opposing position would read this same development as an indication of something else. Since the attempt to identify subject and object is doomed to failure (as Wellek concedes) the Romantic project must be interpreted not on its own terms but rather explained in ways it cannot understand itself. Of these theories one of the most suggestive is that offered by the Marxist account of alienation. Marxism diagnoses the Romantic desire for identification with the object as a symptom of an essentially *compensatory* movement for a loss suffered elsewhere.

A Marxist account of romantic ideology

A starting point for the Marxist understanding of alienation is the assumption (as Marx writes) that production 'not only creates an object for the subject, but also a subject for the object'; that is, through labour the human species creates itself in creating its world, and so, the objective mode of production conditions subjective consciousness. For example, under capitalism, the means of production (factories, offices) are not owned and democratically controlled by the people who work there but by someone else (a private corporation, the state). In this situation the harder you work, the less you create for yourself and the more you make for someone else – people as active and productive subjects become separated from the objective fruits of their labour. Work is experienced as dead time (Monday to Friday) and through a process of compensation 'real life' is felt as what happens on holiday, something personal that takes place on Saturday night and Sunday morning.

In 1923 the Hungarian Marxist, Georg Lukács, worked out a particular application of this theory of alienation for the Romantic movement, a theory which is especially attractive for the case of Wordsworth because Lukács was certainly not writing about him at all. Thus: from the Renaissance through to modern mass-production there is an increasing mechanization and rationalization of the work process, through the introduction of machines, an increasing division of labour and an ever more strict imposition of work discipline. Particularly with industrialization in the period after 1770 the work process is broken down into specialized operations so that no one worker makes the whole finished product, only a part of it. The worker comes to see himself or herself merely as a part or adjunct of the whole process, as, in the language of the time, merely 'a hand'. As the objective process becomes more specialized, rationalized, fragmented and reified, the worker's experience becomes correspondingly the same so that every sense of the interactive wholeness or totality is destroyed.

Lukács regards the philosophy of the Enlightenment as itself a symptom of this loss of rationalization and atomization. And he considers Romantic ideology as a response to and product of the Industrial Revolution. Unable to produce actively for themselves in the objective world, people as subjects in compensation make their field of activity internal and subjective – in Nature, Humanity and Art. Before Romanticism nature had been thought of as ordered, calculable and formal (as in Pope's landscape at Windsor Forest); now, a reversal of meaning emerges (as with Rousseau) and nature becomes, as Lukács says, 'the repository of all these inner tendencies opposing the growth of mechanisation, dehumanisation and reification'.

Nature also comes to refer to a sense of true humanity, people liberated from the false forms of society. And at the same time the status of art changes so as to confer upon the aesthetic a philosophical and ethical weighting it had never previously carried. Since any conception of an interconnected and meaningful totality has been lost in the objective world, the subject expresses itself by seeking an imaginary kingdom in which an image of the whole may be restored. Although there subject and object appear to be reunited, the domain of that apparent unity is itself merely subjective.

Since Marx and Lukács, this kind of historical explanation of Romanticism has been developed by (among others) Christopher Caudwell and Raymond Williams. Such an analysis could point to a whole series of oppositions still prevalent in our society as corresponding to this original split between alienated production and creative consumption: sociologically determined oppositions (work/leisure, factory/home); ideological terms (the political/ the personal, the idea of 'the city'/the idea of 'the country'); philosophic oppositions (fact/value); internal psychic contrasts (reason/emotion, duty/desire) – all of which come to be mapped together and mapped onto a much older opposition between masculine and feminine.

Lukács's account suffers from several limitations. One of the most obvious is that it adheres to what Steve Rigby among others has called 'productive force determinism', an assumption that the development of productive forces exercises a determining influence not only over economic life but over all the rest of culture. So, in the case of Romanticism, Lukács argues that industrialization under capitalism, associated with an increased division of labour in the productive process, explains pretty well everything else that happened at the time. There are all kinds of reasons for doubting this version of determinism, not least that it assumes the social formation to be a totality such that one cause at its supposed centre (the means of production) will have corresponding and even consequences through the whole. Nor does Lukács provide a theory of subjectivity to account for the mechanism by which it all works out as he says. Although these criticisms severely weaken Lukács's causal explanation for Romantic ideology they do not necessarily detract from his insight that such ideology works through a compensatory structure in which an imaginary subjective unity seeks to make good an objective lack.

A psychoanalytic account

Marxist theory privileges a concept of human production, based in the instinct for survival, over the instinct for reproduction, sexuality and the processes of the unconscious. To start at that end of the chain, with reproduction and human society as the expression of unconscious needs and desires, would lead to a very different understanding of Romanticism. Suppose one were to say that every human being in order to perform as a speaking subject must achieve some sense of his or her own identity through recognition from others, then one would view the cultural processes at work in the Romantic period quite another way. Thus, in outline, you could argue that in the typical eighteenth-century village (if it ever existed) the small, relatively closed community reflected back to the individual a strong and relatively stable sense of who he or she was, one to which few alternatives could be imagined. What would be the situation after industrialization and urbanization? Instead of the stable community of agricultural labour there is the wider society in which the individual is socially mobile according to his or her own efforts and abilities; instead of the village, bounded at the horizon by land, there is the city, a seemingly endless metonymy of other houses inhabited by other individuals. In the very movement by which the individual subject is offered an unprecedented range of possible identities, the necessity for an identity fixed by the Other becomes more difficult to satisfy. In consequence, the subject works harder to imagine its way into an autonomous and meaningful identity for itself. Again, it should be noted, a polarizing mechanism is in question.

We should always be on guard against the danger of romanticizing the past but with this caveat I will invoke two writers who have addressed the issue of modernity and individual identity. One is Jacques Lacan:

> What we are faced with . . . is the increasing absence of all those saturations of the superego and ego ideal that are realised in all kinds of organic forms in traditional societies, forms that extend from the rituals ofeveryday intimacy to the periodical festivals in which the community manifests itself . . . It is clear that the promotion of the ego today culminates, in conformity with the utilitarian conception of man that reinforces it, in an ever more advanced realisation of man as individual, that is to say, in an isolation of the soul ever more akin to its original dereliction.

As the communal bonds of traditional society were torn away the subject came to confront ever more nakedly the lack through which it is constituted (its 'original dereliction') and, in consequence, to desire an ever stronger confirmation of its ego.

The other writer is Georg Lukács, from a different work, on the historical novel:

> It was the French Revolution, the revolutionary wars and the rise and fall of Napoleon, which for the first time made history a mass experience, and moreover on a European scale. During the decades between 1789 and 1814 each nation of Europe underwent more upheavals than they had previously experienced in centuries. And the quick succession of these upheavals gives them a qualitatively distinct character, it makes their historical character far more visible than would be the case in isolated, individual instances: the masses no longer have the impression of a 'natural occurrence'.

During this period of crisis people come to see what happens to them as due not to supernatural or 'natural occurrence', not as given, but as humanly constructed in a historical process. This leads to both 'an extraordinary broadening of horizons' and a concomitant passion for an unprecedented sense of nationhood. Again, a compensatory mechanism is at stake: loss of 'natural' identity (in the village, the region) is to be made good in the wish for a new 'cultural' identity as member of a national community.

A reading of William Wordsworth's autobiography, The Prelude, provides a graphic illustration for this kind of experience. As a member of the gentry, with a good education and a degree from Cambridge University, Wordsworth could be expected to enter one of the several professions open at that time to a man of his class who had no inheritance – a lawyer (like his father), a clergyman, possibly an academic. On his own account Wordsworth unhesitatingly dismisses any such thought, already in his first year at university believing that:

> I was not for that hour,
> Nor for that place.
>
> (*III, I: 81–2*)

Instead he becomes a new kind of person, one of the very first intellectuals, committed entirely to unpaid mental labour which he can only live off because he's a member of the gentry. Why?

The question of finding identity in a more fluid society becomes an explicit concern in *The Prelude* and will be mentioned there. First, we may look at a poem from *Lyrical Ballads*, 'A Poet's Epitaph':

> Art thou a Statist in the van
> Of public conflicts trained and bred?
> – First learn to love one living man;
> Then may'st thou think upon the dead.
>
> A Lawyer art thou? – draw not nigh!
> Go, carry to some fitter place
> The keenness of that practised eye,
> The hardness of that sallow face.
>
> Art thou a Man of purple cheer?
> A rosy man, right plump to see?
> Approach; yet, Doctor, not too near,
> This grave no cushion is for thee.

And so this wonderfully sardonic poem unfolds, listing as dead roles all the career options of the gentry in Wordsworth's time, to the politician, the lawyer and the academic here adding the military man, the doctor, the philosopher, and the moralist (but not Stamp Distributor for Westmoreland, the sinecure William Wordsworth finally landed). In tones of the best Augustan satire, measured out in the tightly disciplined and authoritative mode of tetrameter (though rhyming abab), these gentlemen are contemptuously discarded and warned to avoid the dead Poet:

> Shut close the door; press down the latch;
> Sleep in thy intellectual crust;
> Nor lose ten tickings of thy watch
> Near this unprofitable dust.

What Wordsworth has got against them is that they represent: *closure* (shut up because they lack the confidence to remain open); an *unreal surface* (versus a supposedly real depth); *arithmetic* ('ten'); *linear time* ('ten tickings'); *mechanism* (versus the 'organic'); *mastery* (versus open passivity); *profit* (both in the economic and moral sense together). All this is seen as lacking any value at all in contrast to 'the Poet' as imagined in the final verses:

But who is He, with modest looks,
And clad in homely russet brown?
He murmurs near the running books
A music sweeter than their own.

He is retired as noontide dew,
Or fountain in a noon-day grove;
And you must love him, ere to you
He will seem worthy of your love.

The extraordinary fury in this poem follows from absolute faith in the authority with which the dead roles are rejected, giving it a satiric force equal to that of Dryden or Pope (for 'Shut close the door' Wordsworth borrows from the opening line, 'Shut, shut the door, good *John*!', of Pope's 'Epistle to Dr. Arbuthnot'); but the authority is mobilized against the Augustan roles in the name of a Romantic self, the Poet wholeheartedly endorsed because he has been 'an idler in the land'.

The careers and social roles available are equated and spurned because none offers fulfilment for the subjective desires expressed in the figure of the Poet; but that figure correspondingly becomes necessary as a point of identification exterior to and transcending conventional society, since these other denigrated positions have to be excluded. Loss of an acceptable and fixed social identity is to be repaired by constructing an imaginary identity. Again, though on a very different basis to that of the Marxist analysis, the organization of Romantic ideology works through a reciprocal and countervailing strategy in which objective social loss is to be made good subjectively.

It is exactly that sense of a structuring movement William Wordsworth turns to when in 1800 for the 'Preface' to the *Lyrical Ballads* he writes an extraordinarily original passage of cultural critique:

> For a multitude of causes, unknown to former times, are now acting with a combined force to blunt the discriminating powers of the mind, and, unfitting it for all voluntary exertion, to reduce it to a state of almost savage torpor. The most effective of these causes are the great national events which are daily taking place, and the increasing accumulation of men in cities, where the uniformity of their occupations produces a craving for extraordinary incident, which the rapid communication of intelligence hourly gratifies.

Here Wordsworth, struck by an unprecedented cultural change, points to growing social conflict ('great events'), urbanization ('men in cities') and industrialization ('uniformity of their occupations') as leading to 'a craving for extraordinary incident'. Objective social causes produce a subjective effect in a compensatory movement. Growing sensationalism (Wordsworth names not only newspapers but 'frantic novels, sickly and stupid German tragedies, and deluges of idle and extravagant stories in verse') is a desire for a personal intensity that would repair the disappearance of value from society, the city and from work.

His programmatic solution is to write a poetry affirming the inherent and indestructible qualities of human nature which will make up for all this bad stuff, sickly German tragedies, etc. In doing so he has of course already underwritten the opposition in the first place.

This compensatory movement itself constitutes Romantic ideology. And it is because that polarizing structure is still very much alive today that Wordsworth is our contemporary. Even more than him, we inhabit a culture in which loss of meaning in the social reduces it to mere 'fact' supposedly made up for by an increase of 'value' in personal life against which the social is, in turn, confirmed as mere 'fact'. I aim to substantiate these arguments by a reading of the narrative of *The Prelude*, somewhat against its avowed intention.

The Prelude (1850)

There is always a disjunction between signified and signifier in a text, and correspondingly in a narrative, between the narrated (the 'events' of the story) and the narration (the order or performance of narrating those events). While promising to represent the central order of a whole society and time, an epic narrative in the Western tradition frequently operates a special kind of separation between narrated and narration, presenting its narrative *ex post facto*, 'from after the fact'. Thus Virgil's *Aeneid* tells the story of Aeneas and his struggle to found Rome to an audience which already knows that Rome was in fact founded; Dante undertakes his journey through Hell, Purgatory and Paradise already standing firm in a collective certainty that a man will arrive at God's truth about everything, just as Milton sets out to justify the ways of his Protestant God to men (and women) mainly for a readership which already believes those ways justified. Similarly again, in our own time, Brecht's epic play, *Galileo*, achieves authoritative condemnation of the papal opposition to Galileo because now we all know the earth moves round the sun and that Galileo is right. Each epic, then, deploys the difference between narrated and narration to claim an authority for itself: what is narrated as a process of discovery, the narration takes as established fact.

Although William Wordsworth in a letter to George Beaumont (1 May 1805) said that it was 'unprecedented in literary history that a man should talk so much about himself', *The Prelude* has a precedent in Rousseau's *Confessions*. It also draws on Milton's *Paradise Lost* and the epic tradition, for it says something about the general order of its society through a special version of *ex post facto* narrative. In *The Prelude* Wordsworth recounts the process by which he came to see life as necessarily structured by a series of oppositions (between fact and value, the social and the personal, politics and the self, reason and the heart) but he tells it from a position and viewpoint for which those oppositions already seem to be achieved common sense. There's a problem here. If I were to say, 'Let me tell you about the experiences by which I came to the knowledge of what is simply true', then that truth sounds neither so simple nor so true. It's open for someone else to ask, 'If it's just true, how come you had to learn it, and if it's constructed, why is it simply true?' You can re-read the narrative of the experience and point out, 'Of course you say the experience was like that because you are interpreting it, with hindsight, in terms of the way you see things now'. You can argue, as I mean to, that Wordsworth's great series of oppositions was there from the word go. I shall first, in this chapter, retell the story of *The Prelude* from a point of view outside the great oppositions, one which views them as symptoms of a common cause, and then in the next chapters tell that story again, from the inside as it were, in terms of subjectivity.

The Wordsworth of the end of *The Prelude* is sure – and sure his readers in 1850 are sure – that the French Revolution was a mistake. Until a few years ago it seemed obvious he was wrong, and it was possible to tell as a joke the story of the first Premier of the Republic of China, Zhou En-Lai, who was once asked whether he thought the French Revolution was a good thing or not. After considering the long history of his own country, he replied: 'It's too soon to tell'. Now with the undoing of the Soviet Revolution and a widespread willingness to dismiss the very idea that revolution could be a good thing, that joke has lost its point and Wordsworth's attitude towards the outcome of the French Revolution once again takes on plausibility. What has not changed is the way the poem devalues the very possibility of political action, that you might have said to Wordsworth, 'What do you think of the French Revolution?', and he would have replied, 'I had some deeply wonderful personal experiences at that time'.

The first and second books of the poem recreate Wordsworth's early memories, birdsnesting, boat-stealing, skating. Books III and IV are about his education at Cambridge. Book V is about his reading and about death (the account of the boy of Winander is here) but it also contains the poem's first real attempt not just to say what Wordsworth experienced but what it might mean. The statement comes in the form of a dream occasioned by reading *Don Quixote* (not properly understood at the time, the dream's significance emerges retrospectively).

Dreams are not as original and idiosyncratic as we like to think, and Wordsworth's dream is very like some dreamed by Descartes according to Baillet's 1691 *Life of Descartes* (perhaps William Wordsworth, with his interest in mathematics read this or maybe Coleridge told him about it). An Arab appears on a dromedary carrying a stone and a shell; Wordsworth follows him and the Arab says that the stone is Euclid's *Elements of Geometry* and the shell is 'something of more worth', that the end of the world is coming and so he is going to bury the two books, the one that 'wedded soul to soul in purest bond / Of reason' and the other that had voices and power 'to soothe, / Through every clime, the heart of human kind' (V: 104–109). Wordsworth follows him but he gets away as the 'waters of a drowning world' begin to pursue them both. End of dream.

Now there have been lots of different endeavours to interpret this dream. Psychoanalysis suggests that dreams disguise a wish, and may do this best by putting what is most important somewhere it will be least noticed. Among the wishes this dream makes possible is the very belief that founds it, namely the assumption that geometry and poetry, reason and the heart, are necessarily as disjunct and separate as a shell and a stone. Nurtured in Wordsworth's experience as the poem represents it, that opposition lies dormant until it returns to pull him apart in the great personal crisis he has following the French Revolution.

Visiting France for the first time in July 1790 at the age of 20, Wordsworth embraces the Revolution with the famous words:

> But Europe at that time was thrilled with joy,
> France standing on the top of golden hours,
> And human nature seeming born again.
>
> *(VI: 339–41)*

Aside from the 'seeming', it's quite a claim. In this spirit he sees Mont Blanc and interprets it as representing 'genuine brotherhood' and the 'universal reason of mankind' (VI: 545–6). In contrast, living in London after graduating, Wordsworth finds the city entirely false and artificial, merely a performance, a 'moving pageant' (VII: 637), like 'a raree show' (VII: 174). Dr. Johnson said, 'When a man is tired of London, he is tired of life', but for Wordsworth the world's greatest city of the time is a void without meaning or value:

> How oft, amid those overflowing streets,
> Have I gone forward with the crowd, and said
> Unto myself, 'The face of every one
> That passes by me is a mystery!'
>
> *(VII: 626–9)*

Here he experiences, as Raymond Williams says, 'a failure of identity in the crowd of others which worked back to a loss of identity in the self, and then, in these ways, a loss of society itself, its overcoming and replacement by a procession of images'. London confirms to him the insight he had at Cambridge, when, faced with a choice of profession (like those in 'A Poet's Epitaph'), he feels only a sense of vocation, that he was 'not for that hour, / Nor for that place' (III: 81-2), not in fact for any socially realizable hour or place – unless it is contemporary France.

In Books IX–XI Wordsworth narrates his return in 1791–92 to France where he declares himself 'a patriot', a supporter of the revolution, and says 'my heart was all / Given to the people, and my love was theirs' (IX: 124-5). In retrospect he recalls that at the time the success of this unprecedented struggle for political democracy:

> Seemed nothing out of nature's certain course,
> A gift that was come rather late than soon.
>
> *(IX: 246-7)*

In other words, far from seeming unprecedented, the Revolution was simply obvious and natural, a 'progression, not a break', as Robert Young argues. [I find it impossible not to identify strongly with Wordsworth at this point. A personal reminiscence: on 29 March 1968 when I was at the University of Warwick, after the Tet offensive in Vietnam, at the height of the Chinese Cultural Revolution, during the Prague Spring which aimed to produce 'socialism with a human face' and while students and workers were already beginning to take to the streets of Paris, a rumour went round the campus that the lunchtime news would be important; a group of 200 people, including Germaine Greer, Edward Thompson and Catherine Belsey, gathered in front of the television in the students' union; at 1.00 pm Lyndon Johnson announced that because of the anti-war movement he would not be standing for the presidency in the following November; far from being surprised our general feeling was, 'OK, we've got rid of a bad American president – what do we do next?'] In the cities of France Wordsworth shares in a sense of community he missed in London – strangers on the streets were greeted as 'a stranger and beloved as such' (IX: 280).

But . . . the declaration of the Republic is followed immediately in 1792 by the September massacres (X: 48-93) and the Revolution begins to fall apart, leading France into wars of aggression, the Terror of 1793-94 and finally to the dictatorship of Napoleon. Of 1 February 1793, when England declares war on France, Wordsworth says:

> No shock
> Given to my moral nature had I known
> Down to that very moment . . .
>
> (X: 268–70)

In this crisis he is split, divided between England and France, between his home, native culture, family and roots, and his chosen abode, loved ones and the ideals he has consciously and rationally decided for. The war between England and France 'soured and corrupted' his 'sentiments' (XI: 177–8) but still he battles on for some years, trying to make sense of the political situation. Surely reason can do it?

> What delight!
> How glorious! in self-knowledge and self-rule,
> To look through all the frailties of the world,
> And, with a resolute mastery shaking off
> Infirmities of nature, time, and place,
> Build social upon personal Liberty,
> Which, to the blind restraints of general laws,
> Superior, magisterially adopts
> One guide, the light of circumstances, flashed
> Upon an independent intellect.
>
> (XI: 235–44)

But he cannot make sense of it and gives up:

> So I fared,
> Dragging all precepts, judgments, maxims, creeds,
> Like culprits to the bar; calling the mind,
> Suspiciously, to establish in plain day
> Her titles and her honours; now believing,
> Now disbelieving; endlessly perplexed
> With impulse, motive, right and wrong, the ground
> Of obligation, what the rule and whence
> The sanction; till, demanding formal *proof*,
> And seeking it in every thing, I lost
> All feeling of conviction, and, in fine,
> Sick, wearied out with contrarieties,
> Yielded up moral questions in despair.
>
> (XI: 293–305)

To eat or not to eat, to take into your body or expel nourishment, Freud proposes, is the essential model for accepting or rejecting, agreeing or disagreeing. It is sign of the depth of Wordsworth's crisis that it expresses itself in images of good and bad eating: his sentiments are 'soured' as with indigestion, he is 'sick' of the whole question, and when the French people call on an Emperor to save them, it is like 'the dog / Returning to his vomit' (XI: 363–4).

To take in or throw out (and up)? Wordsworth has now two selves, a French identity and an English identity, both of which mean different things for him. He comes back to England to home and family and with time recovers himself:

> Then it was –
> Thanks to the bounteous Giver of all good! –
> That the belovèd Sister in whose sight
> Those days were passed, now speaking in a voice
> Of sudden admonition – like a brook
> That did but *cross* a lonely road, and now
> Is seen, heard, felt and caught at every turn,
> Companion never lost through many a league –
> Maintained for me a saving intercourse
> With my true self . . .
>
> (*XI: 333–42*)

But the 'true' self he recovers is at the price of another self he discards, or, in his own metaphor, sloughs off as a snake does its skin or a person their clothes:

> I had known
> Too forcibly, too early in my life,
> Visitings of imaginative power
> For this to last: I shook the habit off
> Entirely and for ever, and again
> In Nature's presence stood, as now I stand,
> A sensitive being, a *creative* soul.
>
> (*XII: 201–207*)

He gives up social and political hopes, gives up political theory, proof, reason, the intellect as ways to make sense of life. He explicitly makes the choice posed to him by the Arab in the dream, between reason and the heart, what unites a collectivity by election and conscious decision and what holds them together by tradition and instinct, between an apparent outer social role seen as mere custom or learned behaviour ('habit') and an inner self thought to be real, his 'soul'.

It is at this juncture that Wordsworth asserts the view that there 'are in our existence spots of time' (XII: 208), special personal memories constituting individual identity. He goes on to recall two of these, which have been saved till now – when the young Wordsworth was terrified by the name of a murderer inscribed in the turf near a gibbet, when he learned of his father's death. These memorialized personal 'spots of time', rejoin those with which the poem began in Books I and II, so that the order of the narrating of the poem (not its chronological narrative) can begin and end with the personal, containing and enclosing Cambridge, London and France as a kind of digression. Meaningless objective fact or subjective value, empty social role or significant self, reason or the heart: the Wordsworth of *The Prelude* presents these as binary and mutually exclusive opposites. There is, however, another Wordsworth of the 'Preface' to *Lyrical Ballads* who recognizes how such opposites arise from a common origin in the social and historical situation. That Wordsworth sees how modernity brings a loss of significant social identity which can be compensated for in the domain of the self, acknowledges the situation of people for whom 'the uniformity of their occupations produces a craving for extraordinary incident'. In *The Prelude* in contrast, rhetoric and narrative obscure the process of polarization, which produces just that abstracted conception of social 'fact' over against that correspondingly hypostatized sense of personal 'value'.

So there it is. The only thing which lasts, the only source of human meaning, is the stark, self-sufficient I. Yet this assertion of general truth can be read against the grain of its avowed intention. It can be seen (1) to have followed only from one man's particular social and historical experience, an experience which could have been otherwise, and (2) to have been surreptitiously inscribed as the foundation on which the narrative of those experiences could proceed and be interpreted (*either a stone or a shell*).

In the poem ('To William Wordsworth') which he wrote the day after William first read him the manuscript Coleridge spoke of Wordsworth looking out 'calm and sure / From the dread watch-tower of man's absolute self'. Here is how this sense of 'man's absolute self' is articulated, and if it seems to be defending itself against assailing doubts, it should be kept in mind that watch-towers are there only for defence:

> I am lost, but see
> In simple childhood something of the base
> On which thy greatness stands; but this I feel,
> That from thyself it comes, that thou must give,
> Else never canst receive. The days gone by
> Return upon me almost from the dawn
> Of life: the hiding-places of man's power
> Open; I would approach them, but they close.
> I see by glimpses now; when age comes on,
> May scarcely see at all; and I would give,
> While yet we may, as far as words can give,
> Substance and life to what I feel, enshrining,

> Such is my hope, the spirit of the Past
> For future restoration.
>
> (*XII: 273–85*)

Well, we all get older – loss or lack is what makes us speaking subjects. But I would detect here another circle of pathos over and above this, namely that Wordsworth is mourning the impossibility of a transcendent and absolute self which he came to need because society no longer supported a livable sense of identity. When reading Wordsworth's poetry we should keep in mind that this rhetoric of pathos always aims to recuperate, to make good the loss it admits. And that *The Prelude* gives evidence that this deep Wordsworthian mourning originates in the failure of his social hopes.

'All of us one human heart'

So, universal reason is to be dispensed with. And social life, which Wordsworth mistakenly identifies as the particular province of reason, is always subject to casually sardonic dismissal, as what the 'Tintern Abbey' poem terms 'the heavy and the weary weight / Of all this unintelligible world'. Instead *The Prelude* affirms emotional value in 'the depth of human souls' (XIII: 166) and 'the universal heart' (XIII: 220). The rest of Wordsworth's writing has the virtue of keeping faith with this humanist project. What was formerly imaged only in supernatural regions is very deliberately rehoused in this world, not the next:

> Not in Utopia, – subterranean fields, –
> Or some secreted island, Heaven knows where!
> But in this very world, which is the world
> Of all of us, – the place where, in the end,
> We find our happiness, or not at all!
>
> (*XI: 140–45*)

So also in this passage from *The Recluse*:

> Paradise, and groves
> Elysian, Fortunate Fields – like those of old
> Sought in the Atlantic Main – why should they be
> A history only of departed things,
> Or mere fiction of what never was?
> For the discerning intellect of Man,
> When wedded to this goodly universe
> In love and holy passion, shall find these
> A simple produce of the common day.
>
> (*811–19*)

This nicely illustrates Wordsworth's Enlightenment inheritance if it is compared with the opening of Pope's *Windsor Forest* cited before. Both share a firmly secular vision, both assume that traditional classical and Christian paradises can achieve only a natural, not supernatural realization. But if Pope writes as an honest Tory who thinks the bourgeois social order presided over by Queen Anne is the road to human happiness, Wordsworth unfortunately shuts out any social possibility in favour of the merely personal marriage of subject and object, a sense of 'how exquisitely the individual Mind' is fitted 'to the external World' (of which more in the next chapter).

Nevertheless, *The Prelude* and most of Wordsworth's early writing confidently relocates the transcendent from faith in a transcendent object to faith itself, to subjective experience as a domain of transcendence. And its humanism remains similarly committed politically to democracy at least in its parliamentary form. However, the limitations incurred by this position become clear if we consider the sonnet, 'To Toussaint L'Ouverture', who was imprisoned after the failure of a slave rebellion he led in Santo Domingo:

> Toussaint, the most unhappy man of men!
> Whether the whistling Rustic tend his plough
> Within thy hearing, or thy head be now
> Pillowed in some deep dungeon's earless den; –
> O miserable Chieftain! where and when
> Wilt thou find patience! Yet die not; do thou
> Wear rather in thy bonds a cheerful brow:
> Though fallen thyself, never to rise again,
> Live, and take comfort. Thou has left behind
> Powers that will work for thee; air, earth and skies;
> There's not a breathing of the common wind
> That will forget thee; thou has great allies;
> They friends are exultations, agonies,
> And love, and man's unconquerable mind.

Wordsworth's political concern, even after starting *The Prelude*, can extend to a black revolutionary leader, though it can go no further than a definition of politics as the action of one heroic individual (and a defeated one at that). If the best allies Toussaint can call on are air, earth and skies and something blowing in the wind, he's in serious trouble.

3

The Wordsworth Experience

You won't hear me complain –
I'll do my crying in the rain
Popular song

The continuity of the Self

On 26 March 1802 William Wordsworth wrote down this two-sentence poem:

My heart leaps up when I behold
  A rainbow in the sky:
So was it when my life began;
So is it now I am a man;
So be it when I shall grow old,
  Or let me die!
The Child is father of the Man;
And I could wish my days to be
Bound each to each by natural piety.

No other work in the *oeuvre* so perfectly epitomizes so many Wordsworthian themes and effects. It expresses a simple wish that the self continue as a single identity from the past, across the present and into the future so that each moment of time could make up a kind of personal time, in which the days of the calendar and habitual chronology should be 'my days' (not someone else's) 'bound' (not just linked) by a natural unity so that, in a reverse of the usual paternal origin, the experience of the child founds that of the adult man, this unfathered boy somehow originating himself, without dad. Somewhat mysteriously, at least for those new to Wordsworth, the provocation and condition for this desire is an experience in the present in which heart and rainbow, internal and external, seem to coincide spontaneously, one curving upwards (phallicly?) as the other does (from now on I shall refer to this as 'the Wordsworth experience').

God's promise to Noah becomes Nature's promise to Wordsworth. The alternative is death, for if he is not going to go on having this experience he might as well fall into pure unmeaning, 'let me die'. But it is a promise only – that the continuity of the I may be only one possible outcome is acknowledged. The prayer, though in the optative mood ('So be it . . .'), gains credibility from syntactic repetition of what is claimed as a fact ('So was it . . .'). But the fact that it is wished – 'could' be wished for – admits what it would deny: that the continuing identity of the I has to be captured from discontinuities, recuperated from the contingencies of the world and passing time, not to mention a likely weakening of the heart's upward thrust at the sight of a rainbow. In any case (more recuperation), were such intense experiences to fail, they could be recalled, recollections of childhood being still present in the grown-up, the same grown-up, so that personal memory provides a foundation for the sense of a continuing identity.

Further, less noticeable unless we ask 'Who says this?', a speaking voice is represented. This becomes apparent if the poem is recast in the third person:

> His heart leaps up should he behold
>   A rainbow in the sky:
> So was it when his life began;
> So is it now he is a man;
> So be it when he shall grow old,
>   Or let him die!
> The Child is father of the Man;
> And he could wish his days to be
> Bound each to each by natural piety.

This is such a strange thing to say that we would immediately wonder why one man should say it about another, including the wish that he should die, the grasp of this other's inner thought so strong that the speaking voice even knows his secret wish (not quite so surprising if it were 'Her heart' etc., since men are always claiming to know what women are thinking). But it is only a degree less strange that a speaking voice should thus talk about the I represented in the poem, though its effect is clear – even if the I represented fears discontinuity the I speaking may be at one by being at one with it. Of course William Wordsworth is not around to speak the poem and whenever it is read the reader in the present provides the speaking voice and dramatizes the I, obviously enough, though this actuality is generally overlooked, an effect Wordsworth's poetry strongly encourages (more of this in Chapter 7).

A sense of unity between subject and object (the Wordsworth experience), the primacy of individual identity across time, earlier memories, the confidence that I can speak about myself, covert but comprehensive masculinization – pretty well the whole Wordsworthian thematic is encapsulated in these nine lines, though it will take some unpacking. Another example, briefly. For a structure which will generate 'My heart leaps up' would also, if expanded, produce the 'Tintern Abbey' poem, strictly 'Lines' with a subtitling note, 'Composed a few miles above Tintern Abbey, on revisiting the banks of the Wye during a tour. July 13, 1798' (in fact William Wordsworth, the historical author, borrowed the structure from his friend Coleridge who had developed it in 'Frost at Midnight' earlier, in February 1798).

The first paragraph of the 'Tintern Abbey' poem presents the Wordsworth experience, a dramatized affirmation that subject and object, mind and natural world, though distinct, make up a dyadic unity. These 22 lines have been so thoroughly worked over by criticism it is easy to summarize a consensus: reciprocity between subject and object is rendered through a full, flowing syntax that carries easily across between the I and the landscape, often playing between expectations that the words speak of one only for them to end up referring to the other (another example of Wimsatt's romantic wit). At the end of the paragraph it comes as a slight shock to realize the Hermit, sitting alone by his fire in the woods (and clearly a point of identification for Wordsworth), can't be seen, is not in fact objectively described but subjectively imagined ('as might seem'). The particularity of the represented speaker's situation, in space, in time, 'Here, under this dark sycamore', is worked out in the use of the present tense, the first-person singular, demonstratives, even syntax imitating revision in the now – 'These hedge-rows, hardly hedge-rows, little lines / Of sportive wood run wild' – so that the reader is provided with a vivid script to enact an individual thinking and feeling in the present.

This spatial effect of subject/object unity temporally links past and present in Wordsworth's experience. What is happening now is a repetition of what happened five years before:

> Once again
> Do I behold these steep and lofty cliffs,
> That on a wild secluded scene impress
> Thoughts of more deep seclusion . . .

And part of the reason subject/object unity can be claimed is that the remembered image matches what is being seen in the present ('The picture of the mind revives again'). In the second paragraph, the fact of that continuing memory, not consciously solicited but springing spontaneously to mind, is taken to guarantee two things: first, the continuity of the self underneath changing surfaces of conscious social existence, and so, second, something like the meaning of life, when we see 'into the life of things'. It is important that the poem is recounting not an unconscious experience, expressing itself (for example) in dreams, but an experience of the pre-conscious mind, which has a medial position between conscious and unconscious with access to both. So, although the connotations of the poetry here are strongly affective, intonation particularly seeking to represent for the reader a state in which 'we are laid asleep / In body and become a living soul', there is no plunge into unconscious expression. Far from it, in fact, a strong sense of the mastering and controlling I is retained throughout.

After a brief return to the present in paragraph three, the fourth paragraph takes us back to the five-years-gone past, noting difference and change, and so recuperating them in the name of continuity: if I say 'I was different then' the content of my words admits difference while underneath the fact of the statement itself enacts an I able to make this claim who is essentially unchanged. This trope is deployed brilliantly in the lines, 'I cannot paint / What then I was', in which the represented I is said to be unrepresentable while the speaking I – by the very fact of this expression – contrives to give a sense of what it was like before.

Having joined past and present selves into a continuity on the basis of the Wordsworth experience, the speaker now must turn to the future, to the hope that the experience will persist and go on allowing him to feel his unified identity, to the fear that it will fail, and so to the recuperated hope that even if it fails in him it will go on in another so he will still be able to get it at second-hand, as it were. The wish in 'My heart leaps up' that his heart should go on leaping when he's old and that his days be found by 'natural piety' appears in expanded form as a blessing on Wordsworth's sister:

> Therefore let the moon
> Shine on thee in thy solitary walk;
> And let the misty mountain-winds be free
> To blow against thee . . .

As always, it is hard to read this without wondering how she may have felt about being cast in the role of his 'wild thung', subsumed to nature and therefore available for the speaker as an objective point within the Other in which he hopes to see himself reflected.

Starting therefore from 'My heart leaps up' and the 'Tintern Abbey' poem we may analyse how self is affirmed in Wordsworth's poetry, first of all in terms of the now and later in terms of memory. I shall discuss the present in relation to the Wordsworth experience and then the mirroring of the I, so hoping to find a way to make sense of the idea of 'Imagination'.

The Wordsworth experience

We looked at the passage about the boy of Winander as a version of the Wordsworth experience. In a sense almost every poem is predicated on the same thing but more striking examples, besides that in the first paragraph of the 'Tintern Abbey' poem, would be the various childhood experiences recounted in *The Prelude* including birdsnesting (I: 301–339), boat-stealing (I: 357–400), skating (I: 424–63), horse-riding (II: 115–37) and the two deliberately saved for the climax of the poem, the name of the murderer (XII: 225–61) and the death of the father (XII: 287–335), as well as climbing Snowdon (XIV: 11–62). Elsewhere, the Wordsworth experience occurs with a difference (as is hoped for at the end of 'Tintern Abbey') in relation to people, with solitary figures, in 'The Solitary Reaper' for example, and in the 'Lucy' poems, when the experience is married to ideas about gender. In approaching this it should be kept in mind that the perceptual input, the biological and neurological mechanisms, do not determine the experience since the perception can be taken up in lots of different ways, as the earlier discussion of the boy of Winander aimed to show.

Holding on with dear life to grass and rocks while climbing a crag to get at birds' nests the young Wordsworth looks round and suddenly:

> the sky seemed not a sky
> Of earth – and with what motion moved the clouds!
>
> (*I: 338–9*)

Or, while absorbed in skating, he stops and due to vertigo feels (though he knows quite well they don't) that:

> the solitary cliffs
> Wheeled by me – even as if the earth had rolled
> With visible motion her diurnal round!
>
> (*I: 58–60*)

Such passages (and there are many in the works of Wordsworth) are poetic representations of a perceptual effect well known to cognitive psychology. When one *Gestalt* of perception is suddenly replaced by another it is called 'schema shift'. If a subject's attention is preoccupied (in physical effort, for example) and then he or she is forced, suddenly, to review their situation and the world that surrounds them, there can occur a disorienting moment of transition when two schemas briefly overlap.

Our historical author gave an accurate description of schema shift. Referring to the description of the boy of Winander William Wordsworth explained to De Quincey:

> I have remarked, from my earliest days, that, if under any circumstances, the attention is energetically braced up to an act of steady observation, or of steady expectation, then, if this intense condition of vigilance should suddenly relax, at that moment any beautiful, any impressive visual object, or collection of objects, falling upon the eye, is carried to the heart with a power not known under other circumstances.

A subject is caught up in one schema ('steady expectation'); if this schema is replaced by another containing 'an impressive visual object' there is a temporary hesitation between the two. A cognitive shift of this kind would happen to both a human being and an animal, but Wordsworth in his account has already begun to move beyond perception by interpreting what happens in terms of hearts and power. I suggest that the moment of overlap or hesitation is valued because in it the objects in the new schema appear for an instant defamiliarized and, crucially, *unreal*, as a possible fantasy rather than sustained perception:

> the sky seemed not a sky
> Of earth – and with what motion moved the clouds!

('the effect was one of reality seeming unreal' Richard Onorato comments on these lines). If so, the juxtaposition or overlap can be called on to confirm a sense of unity between subject and object (the object, rendered subjectively 'impressive', enters 'the heart'). Wordsworth is well on the way to his preferred interpretation. From this basis I want to review three other ways of interpreting a similar perceptual event.

Geoffrey Hartman in his 1964 book on Wordsworth, after referring to 'The Solitary Reaper', collates and defines the Wordsworth experience as follows:

> A definition can now be offered. The supervening consciousness, which Wordsworth names Imagination in *Prelude VI*, and which also halts the mental traveler in the Highlands, is *consciousness of self raised to apocalyptic pitch*. The effects of 'imagination' are always the same:

a moment of arrest, the ordinary vital continuum being interrupted; a separation of the traveler-poet from familiar nature; a thought of death or judgement or of the reversal of what is taken to be the order of nature; a feeling of solitude or loss of separation. Not all of these need be present at the same time, and some are obliquely present. But the most important consequence is the power itself, whose developing structure is an expressive reaction to this consciousness.

Though this expands on the initial moment to encompass a number of poems and moments from *The Prelude* it begins with what is recognizably the effect of schema shift ('a moment of arrest, the ordinary vital continuum being interrupted'). But it offers a reading of that effect in language and terminology very close to the sort of thing Wordsworth says in his poetry – 'Imagination', 'the order of nature', 'a thought of death', 'a feeling of solitude'.

Is this a reason for simply agreeing to Hartman's reading of Wordsworth and his version of schema shift? I don't think it is, otherwise we could only read Virgil as Roman supporters of the Emperor Augustus, Dante if we were medieval Christians or Pound's *Cantos* if we were fascists. However Wordsworth's poetry might have been read then, in its own time, and even if it seeks to constrain us to that reading, we can't read it the same way now. For we *are* reading it now, for ourselves in the present in changed cultural and historical circumstances (Hartman disavows that fact by claiming the poem itself is 'an expressive reaction' to the Wordsworth experience when the only reaction actually around now is obviously Hartman's while he's reading the poem or ours while we're reading him; it can't be William Wordsworth's since he hasn't been reacting since 1850). Since there is no alternative to reading the poetry now, in other ways than it may have been intended then, we'd better accept the situation. So here are two more theoretical interpretations of the perceptual effect giving rise to the Wordsworth experience.

In *Being and Time* Martin Heidegger develops a distinction between what he terms the 'present-at-hand' (*Vorhanden*) and the 'ready-to-hand' (*Zuhanden*), between things as they are when they are not used by us and things as they are when we appropriate them for what he terms gear or 'equipment' (*Zeug*). If I were making a new pine chair, reached out for my hammer (which is ready-to-hand) and found that unnoticed my Rottweiler had come to sit by the work-bench so that I grasped a wet muzzle instead of a wooden handle, a schema shift would result; and so it would if I went to gather firewood only to be struck by the look of the fir-trees. Heidegger writes:

'Nature' is not to be understood as that which is just present-at-hand, nor as the *power of Nature*. The wood is a forest of timber, the mountain a quarry of rock; the river is water-power, the wind is wind 'in the sails'. As the 'environment' is discovered, the 'Nature' thus discovered is encountered too. If its kind of Being as ready-to-hand is disregarded, this 'Nature' itself can be discovered and defined simply in its pure presence-to-hand. But when this happens, the Nature which 'stirs and strives', which assails us and enthrals us as landscape, remains hidden. The botanist's plants are not the flowers of the hedgerow; the 'source' which the geographer establishes for a river is not the 'springhead in the dale'.

In the moment of lapse when our concern with the ready-to-hand is withdrawn and the present-to-hand is disclosed, Heidegger hints, we may catch a glimpse of Being from the corner of our eye.

Wordsworth certainly wrote about such lapses, what the 'Immortality' Ode names as:

> Fallings from us, vanishings;
> Blank misgivings of a Creature
> Moving about in worlds not realised . . .

There is a respect in which Wordsworth's poetry can throw attention towards Being and the conditions of possibility of what continues to exist, that we could read the Winander boy's 'shock of mild surprise' as an (authentic?) disclosure of his throwness into a world of things (as though it were what Reading 6 in Chapter 1 suggested).

But there are two objections to a Heideggerian reading of Wordsworth along these lines. One is that already entered earlier, with reference to Alain Robbe-Grillet, that the real can never be experienced or perceived as it is, as a Thing which occurs somewhere (and Heidegger is firm in acknowledging this). Another is that the typical movement in Wordsworth's poetry is to admit difference between subject and object only to affirm their interaction and potential unity (a gap or disjunction has to be admitted for unity to be achieved at all). Theory must try somewhere else.

Derealization

Sure enough, Freud's work once again proves its seeming comprehensiveness, for it includes at one point a discussion of what looks very like the Wordsworth experience, as Keith Hanley has acutely perceived. In 'A Disturbance of Memory on the Acropolis' (1936) Freud tells how in travelling he at last reached Athens and there felt 'by the evidence of my senses I am now standing on the Acropolis, but I cannot believe it'. Although he does not stress it, there is a schema shift here, though of a particular kind. One schema comprehends Athens as it is perceived in the present, another Athens as he was taught about it at school. It is, I think, the superimposition of the two which, in cognitive terms, explains Freud's response, 'What I see here is not real', and which he names as a 'feeling of derealisation' (*Entfremdungsdefühl*). However, Freud goes on to propose an account of derealization as an unconscious effect, relating it to the experience of *déjà vu*, and so to the uncanny (in which a present experience is overshadowed by the sense of another scene, this indicating the proximity to it of repressed material). Freud hazards two explanations for derealization, one general, one particular. In general, he suggests, derealization is a form of defence, that to feel the external world is not real is a way of 'keeping something away from the ego' and 'disavowing it'. In particular, he proposes that at least in his own case travel constitutes an expression of dissatisfaction with home, and that his sense of derealization had something to do with 'a child's criticism of his father' – Oedipal antagonism therefore. (I shall concentrate here on the ego, narcissism and defence, leaving the second question – fathers and sons – to be collected in the chapters on autobiography).

There is nothing necessarily attractive about the effect of derealization. In *A Lover's Discourse* Roland Barthes describes what the lover feels while waiting:

> I walk back and forth in my room: the various objects – whose familiarity usually comforts me – the grey roofs, the noises of the city, everything seems inert to me, cut off, thunderstruck – like a waste planet, a Nature uninhabited by Man . . . the world plays at living behind a glass partition; the world is in an aquarium; I see everything close up and yet cut off, made of some other substance; I keep falling outside myself, without dizziness, without blur, without precision, as if I were drugged.

External reality has become unfamiliar, has taken on some of the features of a subjective fantasy as though it were a spectacle. Here a very different and somewhat horrifying interpretation attaches to what Barthes, knowing his Freud, refers to as 'disreality'.

It is – or should be – a remarkable feature in Wordsworth's poetry that Wordsworth mostly welcomes and enjoys this disturbing and potentially uncanny perceptual effect. In *The Prelude* he refers to a moment of 'holy calm' when:

> what I saw
> Appeared like something in myself, a dream,
> A prospect in the mind.
>
> *(II: 350–52)*

Or, again, how roaming Cambridge 'delighted', he finds, 'I was the Dreamer, they the Dream' (III: 30). There are occasions when the hesitation between perception and fantasy comes close to horror, as when he wanders the streets of London and, finding every face 'a mystery', becomes:

> oppressed
> By thoughts of what and whither, when and how,
> Until the shapes before my eyes became
> A second-sight procession, such as glides
> Over still mountains, or appears in dreams . . .
>
> *(VII: 630–34)*

This is much closer to the Barthes example.

Derealization promises a very apt understanding of the Wordsworth experience. For the historical author has produced another little narrative, a very well-known one, which complements his former account of 'the experience':

> Nothing was more difficult for me in childhood than to admit the notion of death as a state applicable to my own being . . . I was often unable to think of external things as having external existence, and I communed with all that I saw as something not apart from, but inherent in, my own immaterial nature. Many times while going to school have I grasped at a wall or a tree to recall myself from this abyss of idealism to the reality.

The word 'idealism' doesn't mean that reality was good but, neutrally, that it appeared non-material, in the sense Berkeley (for example) argued against mind/matter dualism on the grounds that what we perceive as matter is the expression of an idea in the infinite mind of God. Otherwise the story needs little addition. Derealization, the effect of seeing the perceived as fantasy, leads to an overpowering vision of subject/object unity which is associated with life; but this is matched by recognition of the objective status of an external reality over against the I, and this is associated with death.

Cross-referring the perceptual event of schema shift to Hartman's Wordsworthian reading of the Wordsworth experience, to a Heideggerian interpretation, and now to derealization (itself reported in two passages, from Freud and Barthes) should have denaturalized 'the experience'. This enables us to see more precisely how Wordsworth's poetry works, through a process of compression. In a double elision it first aims to present a perception (schema shift) as equivalent to an experience, and, second, to secrete an interpretation inside this experience, all claiming authority from the empiricist gesture of 'this is so, isn't it?' Hartman's paragraph, cited above, is sufficient witness to the strength with which Wordsworth lures us into complicity.

The necessity for a rather heavy-handed argument has been imposed on me by the effort to resist this kind of seductive naturalization (seductive especially for anyone habituated to English culture). I have tried to show how little the perceptual effect of schema shift decides which way it may be constructed as it enters human culture, and in so doing recall that there are in fact no schema shifts in Wordsworth, only the words of the poems. We have to ask what position and fantasy pleasures Wordsworth's staging of subject/object unity may offer to its reader. Once the real is bracketed out, an answer linking such unity to the continuity of the self is not hard to find.

'The Child is father of the Man': these seven words form a perfect epigram for the impossible desire that the subject make itself while writing Daddy out of the script. Impossible, because the subject depends on the Other to confer identity – but not *seeming* impossible if the distinction between perception and fantasy can be blurred, if the Other can be stripped of its alterity, if the object can appear to reflect the subject as 'something not apart from, but inherent in' itself.

Freud's account stresses that in derealization the ego defends itself from what would undermine it. To win a sense of its substantiality and permanence, the identity of the ego must be secured not only as a point in space but also as a position in – and across – time. From the processes of temporality some kind of fixity must be achieved for the I to persist with a (seemingly) continuous identity. Derealization helps the I in two ways. To disavow the otherness of objects retards their threatening flux. But, in the same manoeuvre, upholding correspondence between subject and object helps to establish a point of stability and recurrence beyond the subject in which it may claim to see itself reflected. For subject and object to be felt in reciprocity becomes a condition for asserting the continuity of the self.

Identity was always the urgent topic in the passages and poems we've considered. The boy of Winander calls on the owls to recognize him as one of them, a powerful metaphor. More tellingly, the passage's assertive rhetoric – 'There was a boy' and 'ye knew him well' – attempts to recruit the Other as witness to the boy's existence and identity. If the rainbow's upward curve and the leap of the heart correspond to each other, then the subject's past, present and future are bound into a unity. If the physical landscape of Tintern Abbey is the same for me now as it was five years ago, then it follows I must be the same subject. If my memory of that intense experience springs of its own accord into my mind from the depths of my subjectivity, those depths must be the same now as they were then. The Wordsworthian experience, as Hartman is right to observe, bids to affirm 'consciousness of self' at an absolute limit, subjective identity eternally repeating itself with the least recourse to what is not itself.

The mirroring of the I

There would be no point in arguing that Wordsworth is wrong about the subject/object relation – as Eliot says, once it's got into the poetry, its truth or falsity is no longer really in question. But sooner or later one has to be explicit about one's own stance, and that moment has now been reached. A statement of position serves not to attack Wordsworth's poetry but rather to set up a point at some critical distance from it and so exhibit how it works, how it may be analysed and responded to.

'Who am I?' This seemingly reasonable question hides what it presupposes: that I am an identifiable speaking subject knowing language and so able to ask questions like this. How did I get to be *able* to do that in the first place?

Animals can't do it. Nor can human infants if they are separated from the human community, and this does sometimes happen. Kipling's 'Mowgli' stories of a boy brought up by wolves (and fulfilling the wish that the human subject might be at one with an animal object by learning their language) have a basis in fact. So-called 'feral children' do occasionally turn up, sometimes after being nurtured by wolves or, less flattering to our idea of ourselves, reared by a species which unlike wolves but like us is cheerfully carnivorous as well as herbivorous, pigs. Except of course that feral children don't speak wolf or pig 'language', though they do identify themselves completely with their nurturers, walking on all fours, eating the same food, making the same signals. Such infants (Latin: 'not speaking') can often go on to enter human society, learn to talk, and realize their human potential.

New-born babies don't talk and here Freud is right in saying 'the ego has to be developed'. For to become a speaking subject entails entering language so that I can say 'this' when you refer to the same object as 'that', able that is, to situate myself as an 'I' distinct from the world and other people in it. Why should we have the potential to do this but a potential which necessitates the human Other for its realization? What inherited need compels us to seek an identity in the human community? If one imagines what it is like to be an infant the most plausible answer is hardly surprising. There you are (or rather not 'you', not yet) encompassed by terrible and wonderful powers on whom you are utterly dependent but which you cannot even name as 'terrible' or 'wonderful'. It's obvious you most want to be one of them.

According to the Lacanian account 'I am a hole surrounded by something': the human subject originates not in presence and identity but rather in lack or absence. We define ourselves as human in the impossible task of fantasizing ourselves as complete, desiring (and thinking we find) a plenitude which will make good that originary lack (originary? Lacan points to the fact that the newborn of our species is premature, always cast out from the Edenic womb *too soon*). The discourse of the Other promises to make up for this. For Lacan my identity begins as a unified likeness reflected back from everyone else (beginning, no doubt, with the parent who hails the baby into language – 'aren't you a little sweetie?'). Mirrored by those who love me, having nowhere else to go and terrified that my body is in pieces (what was it bumped so painfully into that chair? whose head? my head?), I have to identify myself in – and as – what the Other desires me to be. My identity, then, is not something I recognize because that would suppose I was already there able to do the recognizing: I come about in a dialectic between the subject and the Other, by winning from it a relatively fixed position I can call my own – me. Unreal, fictional, this kind of I, achieved in exchange with the Other, is the only one I can ever have.

No-one can escape the subject/object dialectic which compels us, if we wish to speak coherently, to appropriate a place from within the Other in whose temporary stability we may find a voice. In connection with Wordsworth it is a question of the degree and kind of the position wished for. On the Isle of St Pierre, watching the placid lapping of the water on the shore, Rousseau asks:

> What does one experience in a state like this? Nothing outside oneself, nothing except oneself and one's own being – as long as that state lasts, one is sufficient to oneself, like God.

Wordsworth's self wants to occupy all the available space there is and would really like to have made himself, as apparently God the Father has contrived to do in *Paradise Lost*. At one point Adam feels desire for another, for he doesn't know what, and asks God for a wife. This may be a mistake because, unlike Zeus, the Christian God eschews the normal decencies of sexual intercourse, is not himself married, and so teases Adam by pretending to take the question as a slur on His Own single status:

> What thinkst thou then of mee, and this my State,
> Seem I to thee sufficiently possest
> Of happiness, or not? who am alone
> From all Eternitie, for none I know
> Second to mee or like, equal much less.
>
> (VIII: 403–407)

Deities aside, the ordinary human self can only be there if it is there for the Other, loved by the other. Knowing this, Wordsworth wishes to make the best of a necessarily bad job by reducing dependence on the Other to the least possible.

But there is a real problem here, as anyone will know who has ever loved a dog. The good news is that once properly trained your spaniel will mirror your every mood and inflection with undying adoration but the bad news is that as representative of the Other even the most cuddly creature, mouth wet with love, can only recognize you from an animal's point of view (its instincts are forcing it to respond to you as a surrogate pack-leader). So Hamm in Beckett's *Endgame* wants his servant Clov to leave his dog (breed unspecified) 'standing there imploring me'; Clov agrees, but Hamm is blind and can't see the dog has actually fallen over (it was stuffed anyway). In a similar scenario, Wordsworth will settle for recognition by a tree, a lake or a mountain, but only on condition he can somehow blank out the reality principle, his consciousness that it is only a material object after all. That condition can be partly met if he is in a sufficient state of excitement to forget what's really happening. An animal might be better because it is after all a member of a species in some ways like our own though few poems attempt this strategy (there is the odd bird, especially the cuckoo).

It would be best, of course, to be loved and recognized by someone who is human and whose love is therefore really worth having. But here the problem is that, being human, the other human being will want their own share of recognition from you. What makes your partner more desirable than a Pekinese as witness is precisely what makes him or her less consoling and reliable than a Pekinese. It's like the contradiction everyone knows Groucho Marx expressed perfectly: 'I don't want to be a member of any club that would have me as a member'. Even so, inevitably, Wordsworth does call on other human beings to recognize him but has a number of strategies with which he tries to neutralize their own desires and reduce the risk of them looking at him and demanding recognition from him.

One is to use children. They obviously count as human, so being preferable to dogs, and have the advantage that they are unlikely to make too many demands on an adult stranger. Another, for much the same reason as far as Wordsworth is concerned, is to use women, like the sister in the 'Tintern Abbey' poem (there is a separate chapter on this tactic). If an adult male is called on as witness, a consistent strategy is to choose this stand-in for the Other outside any normal human social context, outside the city, away from manners and obvious conventions, on the road, in the countryside, alone. So there is a whole army of solitary individuals the poet encounters – shepherds, discharged soldiers, old Cumberland beggars, children who won't admit their siblings are dead, and so on. Although it is easy to mock this, one effect is that it is meant to be mocked so that the reader will not notice too easily how much a position in the Other is being appropriated by the self. Often the solitary figure is silent, like Michael in the poem of that name, who had been:

> alone
> Amid the heart of many thousand mists,
> That came to him, and left him, on the heights.

But the same contradiction applies again: if the figure is silent, reduced in its humanity, then it ends up not much better suited as a way to get yourself loved than a Dalmatian.

Another move, then, is to make the figure a speaking subject, situated within meaning therefore, but not to listen to what he or she says. The Leech-gatherer in 'Resolution and Independence' is at first barely animate, 'a huge stone', but gradually emerges 'like a sea-beast' and finally responds to the speaker's question about what he does for a living. But the speaker is miles away:

> The old Man still stood talking by my side:
> But now his voice to me was like a stream
> Scarce heard; nor word from word could I divide;
> And the whole body of the Man did seem
> Like one whom I had met with in a dream . . .

Or, if it is a speaking subject, they can be themselves self-absorbed (in their work, for example) so that their own gaze is turned, as it were, on themselves; or they can speak a foreign language, not understood by the subject who observes them. Both these last manoeuvres are combined in a poem about a woman seen in Scotland.

'The Solitary Reaper'

The look by which the speaker solicits the other's recognition ('love me!') is similar to that of the aesthetic gaze which treats something as an object for pleasure and contemplation. There is therefore a certain irony when the person selected as representative of the Other is herself working, as is the woman in 'The Solitary Reaper' (there is even a little touch of eros in the fact that she is 'bending' over):

> Behold her, single in the field,
> Yon solitary Highland Lass!
> Reaping and singing by herself;
> Stop here, or gently pass!
> Alone she cuts and binds the grain,
> And sings a melancholy strain;
> O listen! for the Vale profound
> Is overflowing with the sound.
>
> No Nightingale did ever chaunt
> More welcome notes to weary bands
> Of travellers in some shady haunt,
> Among the Arabian sands:
> A voice so thrilling ne'er was heard
> In spring-time from the Cuckoo-bird,
> Breaking the silence of the seas
> Among the farthest Hebrides.
>
> Will no one tell me what she sings? –
> Perhaps the plaintive numbers flow
> For old, unhappy, far-off things,
> And battles long ago:
> Or is it some more humble lay,
> Familiar matter of today?
> Some natural sorrow, loss, or pain,
> That has been, and may be again?
>
> Whate'er the theme, the Maiden sang
> As if her song could have no ending;
> I saw her singing at her work,
> And o'er her sickle bending: –
> I listened, motionless and still;
> And, as I mounted up the hill,
> The music in my heart I bore,
> Long after it was heard no more.

The woman is close to being as passive as she could be while remaining articulate; she works, 'bending' over, while he (it is a he) looks at her, unobserved; he feels sorry for her and supposes he identifies with her in terms of a universal human nature (her song is – is imagined by him to be – about 'some natural sorrow, loss or pain'). This is the Wordsworth experience. When faced with a strange otherness, another subject but one whose attention is wholly directed inwards, a speaking subject but one separated from him by language, a woman while he is a man, a labourer though he is a gent, a Scot when he is English, the speaker is frozen for a second at a loss. However, through an act of identification he is able to make her over reassuringly into part of himself so he can carry away a little image of her 'in my heart'. Song – art – supposedly mediates between subject and object, making good all the oppositions and differences just mentioned.

Yet what he really identifies with is not her but rather the image of himself as the noble, uplifted and sympathetic lover of humanity, the image which her song is taken to reflect back to him and for which her otherness is used as support and guarantor. An indication of this is his demand that we as readers should 'Behold her' though in practice he is calling on us to behold him being high-minded.

It is, alas! exactly what the two American college-boys, James Agee and Walker Evans, saw, photographed and wrote about after living among sharecroppers in the 1930s in their book, *Let Us Now Praise Famous Men*, a position which Agee tries but fails to escape when he says with deliberately savage irony that the book 'is written for all those who have a soft place in their hearts for the laughter and tears inherent in poverty viewed at a distance'. It is the look of the first world at what it terms 'the third world' under the cliché of 'starving babies in Africa', the look and gesture of charity (Live Aid and its successors) which, in Freud's scandalous suggestion, is only given because it allows the giver to enjoy their superiority over the recipient ('Leave him like that, standing there imploring me', says Hamm of his dog).

I would like to know what the woman is singing in Wordsworth's poem and would be encouraged if it were something ribald. In 1977 the German film director, Leni Riefenstahl, spent time in the Sudan photographing Nubian body-painters, and very beautifully they were photographed too. A couple of years later the BBC showed a film made about the same body-painters by an anthropologist who spoke Nubian, and one sequence had subtitles in which one man says, 'I've forgotten how to do this stuff', and his older companion replies, 'It doesn't matter, it's only for the fucking tourists'. In 'The Solitary Reaper' the woman's point of view, her suffering, her work, her otherness has to be effaced, and the conditions of contemporary Western society make this appropriating gaze very hard to elude. However, some redress is made in a poem, 'A Highland Woman', by Sorley Maclean which comes almost as a deliberate riposte to Wordsworth:

> Hast thou seen her, great Jew,
> who art called the One Son of God?
> Hast Thou seen on Thy way the like of her
> labouring in the distant vineyard?
>
> The load of fruits on her back,
> a bitter sweat on brow and cheek,
> and the clay basin heavy on the back
> of her bent poor wretched head.
>
> Thou hast not seen her, Son of the carpenter,
> who art called the King of Glory,
> among the rugged western shores
> in the sweat of her food's creel.
>
> And every twenty Autumns gone
> she has lost the golden summer of her bloom,
> and the Black Labour has ploughed the furrow
> across the white smoothness of her forehead.
>
> And Thy gentle church has spoken
> about the lost state of her miserable soul,
> and the unremitting toil has lowered
> her body to a black peace in a grave.
>
> And her time has gone like a black sludge
> seeping through the thatch of a poor dwelling:
> the hard Black Labour was her inheritance;
> grey is her sleep to-night.

This does not entirely escape the mastery of the aesthetic gaze and the fact that it is speaking for the woman, and perhaps it knows that it can't (the slight but deliberate exaggeration of 'poor wretched head'?). But it brilliantly displaces that look sideways by attributing it to Jesus, his look ('Hast Thou seen her . . .') and his obsession with the state of her 'miserable soul', thus opening a space for her experience and the 'Black Labour' to speak for itself.

The terms of the dialectic between self and Other might be summed up at this point as follows. The more like you the representative of the Other is, the better the other can love you; but the more it is like you, the more it will make its own claim on your recognition.

Wordsworth, then, does try to play the game of recognition using a rising scale of natural, animal, childish and adult human figures. But these merely stand in for the Other, to make sure it is admitted at all. They are not the images which the I desires to see itself as, far from it. As 'The Solitary Reaper' instances, that image is rather something projected from the speaker, a position in the scenario between the imaginary I that looks and the object looked at. But if that is the case, why not try to miss out the Other altogether? Why not let the game take place between one version of yourself and another? Why play with the Other when you may get on just as well by playing with yourself? In Wordsworth's autobiographical poems this is the main strategy.

—4—
Autobiography 1: Theme

HAMM (proudly):
But for me,
(*gesture towards himself*)
no father. But for Hamm,
(*gesture towards surroundings*)
no home.
(*Pause*)

Samuel Beckett
Endgame

Truth in autobiography

A narrative of the life of the great man – more rarely woman – was a genre known to the ancient world. Aside from the *Confessions* of St. Augustine, representation of the individual life remained essentially a record of the role he or she played in society until late in the eighteenth century, and this is the form taken by Edward Gibbon's *Memoirs* as late as 1796. Completed in 1765 and published in 1781, Rousseau's *Confessions* transformed the terms in which personal life could be conceived by moving attention inwards, to a narrative radically at odds with the external biographical facts. The idea of 'confession' linked this kind of narrative back to the sacrament of penance made individual and obligatory by the Lateran Council in 1215; Wordsworth referred to *The Prelude* as the poem about the growth of a poet's mind; and in 1809 Robert Southey was the first person to use the word 'autobiography' (*OED*, 2nd edn).

Unlike that of most other literary genres the discourse of autobiography claims to correspond to the real. As Elizabeth Bruss says, 'Information and events reported in connection with the autobiographer are asserted to have been, to be, or to have potential for being the case'. *The Prelude* clearly purports to represent in the poem aspects of the life of the historical William Wordsworth (1770–1850). Coupled with the rather literal-minded assumptions about authorial intention made by conventional criticism, the autobiographical feature has led to discussion of where and in what respects the poem is telling the truth about Wordsworth. Here are some examples.

What is the chronology of the opening section which appears to refer to William Wordsworth's move to Racedown in 1795 but also to his settling in Grasmere in 1799? In London did he visit Bartholemew's Fair in 1791 or 1792? Notoriously, while he claims to have seen armed men occupying the Grande Chartreuse in August 1790 (*The Prelude*, VI: 414ff.), it is historical fact that this did not happen until May 1792 (and it is not mentioned in the 1805 version). The passage in which he recalls finding a gibbet and the name of the murderer cut in the grass has in particular attracted dispute. There is no reference to letters in the grass in the 1798–99 version of the poem. Jonathan Wordsworth quotes the 1805 version and comments:

> 'The monumental writing was engraven / In times long past' – Thomas Nicholson, the murderer in question, had been hanged for killing a local butcher in August 1767, only two and a half years before the urchin's birth. The letters, even if carved very 'soon after that fell deed was wrought', were at most seven or eight years old; the gibbet, unless made of remarkably inferior wood, would not even have fallen, much less 'mouldered down'. For all the circumstantial detail, we are dealing not with fact, but with poetry of the imagination.

These examples show that it is possible to argue seriously with *The Prelude* over matters of fact, just as there is a serious debate over passages in the *Confessions* when Rousseau is, at best, being economical with the truth, at worst, deliberately lying so as to make himself look good.

There is and can be no categorical opposition between works of fact and works of fiction. Documentary texts must construct whatever version of truth they offer on the basis of discourse and simply cannot insulate their textual operation against a fictional reading. On the other hand, an *absolutely* fictional text would be inconceivable, one in which there was not a single accurate fact, not even that Paris is the capital of France and people have one head and two legs rather than vice versa. Moreover, what counts as a factual or fictional text is decided by the

historical consensus of a given society (ours adheres to a fierce demarca-
tion between the kinds).

Even the most thoroughly documentary text, precisely because it
is textual, must be open to the effects of identification and fantasy.
For example, on 25 September 1991 the lunchtime television news
(BBC 1) reported live the return to England by air of a hostage held
in Lebanon, Jackie Mann, to be greeted by his wife and the fly-past
of a Supermarine Spitfire (such as Mann had flown in 1940 when he
was a Second World War fighter pilot). I doubt whether a single fact
in this outrageously protracted 25 minutes of coverage was actually
invented but a very enticing scenario was offered to the imagination. As
the past was relived in the present and the previously missing pilot was
returned to his steadfastly plucky and gracious wife – he still sporting a
handlebar moustache, she looking like a septuagenarian Vera Lynn (the
Forces Sweetheart) – this news report fulfilled many of the same wishes
as the scene in 'Close Encounters of the Third Kind' when all those lost
people come down from the hold of the visiting craft. Truth does not
keep a text immune from desire.

Since documentary cannot but supply the pleasures of fiction, since,
as Robert Elbaz asserts, 'the autobiographer always writes a novel, a
fiction, about a third person' which is enjoyed as such, it's fair to ask
what effects result from the truth-claims of autobiography. One is
clearly the function of rationalization, to give a logically consistent or
ethically acceptable justification for feelings whose unconscious motives
are not perceived. Dreams, as psychoanalysis asserts, disguise wishes
by expressing them in a revised form; one form that revision may take
is a dream in which at a certain point one finds oneself aware 'This is
only a dream' or 'This dream is like a movie'. It is through a similar
process of revision and rationalization that people enjoy the pleasures
of fantasy while thinking they are only reading what is true. Biography
and autobiography, two very popular forms of contemporary reading,
provide many of the same pleasures as fiction, including identification
with a heroic, successful and desirable man or woman.

A second function of truth in autobiography follows from it being
a historical text (even if, as in Wordsworth's case, the history is within
living memory). A historical text may describe what has happened in
the form of present events and choices (Aeneas founding Rome, General
Custer fatally dividing the command into three sections prior to the
Battle of Little Big Horn). Just as the historical text lends a connotation
of necessity to what it describes through the reader's prior knowledge
that it has happened, so the autobiographical text confers a sense of
destiny on what the autobiographer reports. What he or she reports

mingles documentary fact in with personal memory. And memory is a difficult matter.

Memory

In Ridley Scott's film, 'Blade Runner', set in 2019, the task of a Blade Runner is to terminate humanoid robots (Replicants) who have exceeded their four years' working life. Some advanced-model Replicants have been programmed with memories and have come to think of themselves as human. These resist termination. One plangent sequence shows the Blade Runner brutally confronting a beautiful female Replicant, Rachel, with the fact that her most intimate early memories – playing 'you show me yours' with the boy next door, the spider whose eggs took all summer to hatch and when they did they ate her – have in fact been implanted into her by her manufacturer, Tyrell, who has borrowed them from his daughter. No doubt the sequence gives a new twist to an old piece of gender ideology ('men are for real, women can fake') but it also awakens the most profound threat to human identity: if my memories are not mine how can I know who I am – how indeed can I be sure I am an I at all? Another example, a personal one. Born at the start of the Second World War in Portsmouth I have an early memory of one night surprising a sailor and a woman secreted together on an overgrown bomb-site. I assumed this was a private and unique experience so it was unnerving for me to see the film 'Hope and Glory' and find an identical incident in it (did every child of the Blitz, I wonder, collect a similar version of the primal scene?). If my memory can be shared with someone else – in a word, replicated – how can it be mine?

Clearly the body changes over time – does the identity of the self? John Locke, writing in 1690, considers personal memory to be constitutive of individual identity. Assuming consciousness to be self-consciousness, Locke asserts that identity continues even if the substance of the body changes:

> For it being the same consciousness that makes a Man be himself to himself, personal Identity depends on that only, whether it be annexed only to one individual Substance, or can be continued in a succession of several Substances. For as far as any intelligent Being can repeat the Idea of any past action with the same consciousness it had of it at first, and with the same consciousness it has of any present Action; so far it is the same personal self. For it is by the consciousness it has of its present Thoughts and Actions, that it is a self to it self now, and so will be the same self, as far as the same consciousness can extend to Actions past and to come . . .

On this showing (David Hume has a much more uncertain notion of self-identity) I am the same person if I can repeat a memory with the same consciousness now as I had of it then. Among the many big questions that loom over this issue (on which something must be said since the issue is directly relevant to Wordsworth's presentation of the self), one is, 'If I repeat a past idea, how can it be the same as it was the first time?' (a problem which will recur in this present discussion), and another is, 'How can I tell a memory from a fantasy?'

Memories and fantasies have at least the following in common: they consist of little scenes or scenarios in which the subject figures; they can only be experienced in the present; they are both motivated by desire (a memory becomes a memory – is remembered – either because a feeling of pleasure has got attached to it or because the subject wants to master a painful memory). But while memories pertain to the past, fantasies project hopes and fears into the future. Memories thus intersect with the real in a way fantasies do not; the act of remembering is an expression of desire and so is the act of having a fantasy but, because of this relation to the real, memories are more *resistant* to desire (the reader might test this by running their preferred fantasy against their favourite memory).

Time is the most difficult question of all. What really makes any distinction between memory and fantasy fraught in the extreme is that it's entangled with the issue of temporality. Both memories and fantasies can only be entertained in the present; since both are expressions of desire, a memory will constantly pick up new meanings and associations from each occasion on which it is recalled, in a process which is interminable. If a memory is like a stone skipping across the surface of consciousness, it is changed each time it touches the surface while also reciprocally changing that consciousness. Freud discusses this effect in terms of *Nachträglichkeit*, deferred action or interpretation. For example, the infant, after experiencing loss of the breast at the oral stage, encounters the possibility of castration in the later, genital stage, and retrospectively interprets weaning as an anticipation of the threat to sexual pleasure. As Freud says, while discussing the putative memories of one of his most unfortunate patients, referred to as 'Wolf Man':

> I admit that this is the most delicate question in the whole domain of psychoanalysis. I did not require the contributions of Adler or Jung to induce me to consider the matter with a critical eye, and to bear in mind the possibility that what analysis puts forward as being forgotten experiences of childhood (and of an improbably early childhood) may on the contrary be based upon phantasies created on occasions late in life.

Because of deferred action, any firm opposition between memory and fantasy simply dissolves; the subject is constructed in an endless dialectic between past and present, without terminus or point of origin. This is a most delicate question for Freud, but so it is also for Wordsworth and our readings of his work.

We should therefore not hesitate to draw on psychoanalysis in trying to understand Wordsworth's dramatization of memory and remembering. Cognitive psychology can indicate some general mechanism in human memory which prefers items in simply opposed categories and tends to discard those which do not classify easily. This doesn't get us very far. Psychoanalysis, on the other hand, foresees a dynamic of identity and self-identification at work within the process of memory – for Freud as much as for Wordsworth the child is parent of the adult.

Coleridge in Chapter 7 of *Biographia Literaria* carries out a sustained argument with the psychology of his day over the question of how ideas came to be associated in the mind. Hobbes, Locke and Hume among others had attempted to describe laws of association by which ideas were linked in the memory as a consequence of various factors external to the subject (simultaneity, contiguity, cause and effect, resemblance, contrast), all of which Coleridge assigns to the single classification of contemporaneity (i.e. two things linked because they were experienced at the same time). He dismisses this account, arguing that ideas are linked according to an internal principle and concluding that 'the true practical general law of association is this; that whatever makes certain parts of a total impression more vivid or distinct than the rest, will determine the mind to recall these in preference to others equally linked together by the common condition of contemporaneity'. In other words, out of all the things that happen to us at a certain moment we give preference in our memories to what we want to remember. And this is exactly what Freud proposes. Losing the actual pleasure of being suckled, for example, we retain an image of the breast because it is associated with pleasure rather than unpleasure. And the identity of the subject beyond its social role derives from such choices, memories and recollections, and without them it could not support its socially assigned position.

'Spots of time'

Wordsworth is not writing about memory as a conscious, willed operation. Rather, his concern is with memories that spontaneously come to mind because they are linked with a feeling of pleasure, as Coleridge recognizes. The second paragraph of the 'Tintern Abbey' poem stages the memories of that landscape not as some fixed and mechanical record but as an active and continuing intervention entering reflective consciousness of its own accord from somewhere else, importing:

> that serene and blessed mood,
> In which the affections gently lead us on, –
> Until, the breath of this corporeal frame
> And even the motion of our human blood
> Almost suspended, we are laid asleep
> In body, and become a living soul . . .

We are talking about memories which persist and 'arise' (a typical word) yielding a quasi-mystical, trance-like state, clearly unconscious or pre-conscious in origin. *The Prelude* expands – and enacts – a view of the continuity of personal memory which takes it as a transcendental guarantee of individual identity.

In one respect, as Locke proposes, it is a simple truth that if a person could not remember a past which, to some degree, belonged only to them, they would have no individual identity. I shall suggest, however, that Wordsworth asserts a would-be absolute sense of personal identity which aims to exclude any acknowledgement of its dependence on the Other, a sameness which would renounce all difference, even though, in the conditions of contemporary Western culture, we seem to be unable to do without this projection of selfhood to give life meaning.

In *The Prelude*, after passages describing how he recovered from the French Revolution and found his 'true self' once again, Wordsworth talks about memory and identity. Exposition is sandwiched between illustration. First there is the assertion that special personal memories constitute 'spots of time':

> There are in our existence spots of time,
> That with distinct pre-eminence retain
> A renovating virtue . . .
> > Such moments
> Are scattered everywhere, taking their date
> From our first childhood.
>
> > (*XII: 208–225*)

This is followed by a memory: coming across a gibbet with a murderer's name carved in the turf alongside the young Wordsworth fled in terror to the top of the moor which he felt as a 'visionary dreariness' (XII: 225–71). Then there is a more discursive passage when he exclaims:

> Oh! mystery of man, from what a depth
> Proceed thy honours. I am lost, but see
> In simple childhood something of the base
> On which thy greatness stands; but this I feel,
> That from thyself it comes, that thou must give
> Else never canst receive. The days gone by
> Return upon me almost from the dawn
> Of life: the hiding-places of man's power
> Open; I would approach them, but they close.
> I see by glimpses now; when age comes on,
> May scarcely see at all; and I would give,
> While yet we may, as far as words can give,
> Substance and life to what I feel, enshrining,
> Such is my hope, the spirit of the Past
> For future restoration.

> (XII: 273–86)

Finally, in a move which could hardly be more weighted, he concludes the book with another 'memorial', saved out of chronology to be inserted here: the death of his father (XII: 287–335). Although this all appears common sense to us at first sight, only a fairly complex analysis can show how it is meant to work.

Privileged memories are 'spots of time'; though lost in actuality, these can be recollected through memory; remembering in the present impressive events from one's past is felt to affirm the continuity of the individual self, and so its identity. There would appear to be four conditions for this affirmation:

1 There is the traditional Western conception of continuous-homogeneous or linear time modelled on a conception of space, time as a continuous succession of identical units (the now) accumulating remorselessly into seconds, minutes, days, years, centuries and so on *ad infinitum* (!).
2 This kind of temporal structuring is internalized to give an inner space for subjectivity in opposition to what is now seen as external, chronological time.
3 But not all of the units of this inner space – not every single memory – counts as a personal unit, for particular ones extracted from the (almost) endless line stretching into the dim past gain special status as 'spots of time'. Like old photographs, these are punctual, that is, they have the same attributes as the line from which they are extracted being both points in time and places in space. The notion of time as a 'spot' changes temporality into geography, making it a position at which one is present. So contingent memories are relegated in

favour of others deemed to be necessary in and for the self, early memories in particular.

4 Finally, because in the first place these 'spots of time' are shaped as spatio-temporal units, like photographs again, they can be looked at – the I in the present can see them as objects, and so (in the process the previous chapter sought to make familiar) the I can see itself reflected in these memories of itself.

It has to be said that none of this will work:

1 If time does not consist of spatio-temporal units but of nows only defined by their relation to each other.

2 If the opposition between external and internal time cannot be sustained (when, for example, time is thought of not as a binary of this kind but as an uneven bundle of different temporalities).

3 If the distinction between ordinary and special (contingent and necessary) memories breaks down.

4 If, because of *Nachträglichkeit*, past memories cannot be construed as a kind of object, a 'spot' or 'memorial', but have to be understood as caught up in present fantasies which *transform them every time they are recalled*. Why is this worth pursuing? Because if the self has no point of origin in childhood and no end in adult 'greatness', if it does not 'stand, (like a substance or an entity) but consists of a process, an interminable dialectic in which each memory is rewritten (however slightly) on every occasion it is remembered, then it is only the inter-subjective Other of social life which can confer stable identity on the self (and a provisional stability at that).

At least we now have reason to think otherwise of Wordsworth's account of memory. Strictly, only the two memories placed in Book XII are 'spots of time' though it seems clear the notion is meant to extend to a whole series of memories strung together across *The Prelude*. These include early memories, some generalized, such as that of the stream Wordsworth grew up by (I: 269ff.), but also particular events that are narrated, notably:

> birdsnesting (*I: 306ff.*)
> stealing a boat (*I: 356ff.*)
> skating (*I: 425ff.*)
> horse-riding (*II: 55ff.*)

as well as the two saved till Book XII. Among later memories which could qualify as privileged moments would be the time he stayed up all night and at dawn came to feel that he was 'A dedicated Spirit' (IV: 337), meeting a discharged soldier (IV: 370ff.) as well as:

his dream of the Arab-Quixote (*V: 50ff.*)
the boy of Winander (*V: 364ff.*)
the drowned man (*V: 426ff.*)
crossing the Alps (*VI: 557ff.*)
the blind beggar in London (*VII: 630ff.*)
the shepherd (*VIII: 256ff.*)

And there are others which might be added to this list. For Wordsworth's account of memory and identity to work plausibly these separated 'spots of time' must add up to a coherent unity – the reader must feel a single thread runs through these jewelled moments. 'The Child is father of the Man': Wordsworthian identity is based in 'simple childhood', and it is in the pattern of the early memories that the structuring of unified identity can be discerned.

Early memories

Records of early memories are not unusual, this for instance from Leonardo da Vinci:

> It seems that I was always destined to be so deeply concerned with vultures; for I recall as one of my very earliest memories that while I was in my cradle a vulture came down to me, and opened my mouth with its tail, and struck me many times with its tail against my lips.

Leonardo's strange little scene is written down in his manuscripts and this is how Freud recounts it in *Leonardo Da Vinci and a Memory of his Childhood*. Rousseau records three early memories – interposing his own body to stop his father beating his brother, peeing in a neighbour's cooking-pot while she was at church, the tune of a song whose words he has half-forgotten – but he doesn't attribute much significance to them.

Coleridge in 'Frost at Midnight' is among the first to provide a poetic representation of early memory, one to which he ascribes determining value:

> But O! how oft,
> How oft, at school, with most believing mind,
> Presageful, have I gazed upon the bars,
> To watch that fluttering *stranger!*

Nothing is ever straightforward with Coleridge, and here the poem refers to a superstition that a certain flame on the grate means someone unexpected will arrive. The poem goes on to disclose another childhood memory within this memory:

and as oft
With unclosed lids, already had I dreamt
Of my sweet birth-place, and the old church-tower,
Whose bells, the poor man's only music, rang
From morn to evening, all the hot Fair-day,
So sweetly, that they stirred and haunted
With a wild pleasure . . .

This early (is it earliest?) memory recalls a special occasion, the Fair, when the bells rang all day in the extraordinary summer heat. 'Frost at Midnight' makes it clear the moment is valued because the heat and prolonged music of the bells effect a sense of unity between subject and object, anticipating a feeling that God teaches 'Himself in all, and all things in himself'.

Psychoanalysis has a careful account of early memories, which it terms *screen memories*, and this goes a long way to explain the criteria by which some memories are selected and treated as necessary to some general cohesion or order peculiar to a self. Freud first makes the fascinating but commonsense observation that even children as young as three or four have a highly organized mental functioning and know what they're doing but that human memory fades as we try to go back from around 10 or 12 years old, becoming very patchy indeed in the earlier years. Further, we might expect that important events would be selected as worth remembering. In fact, many early memories are not like this at all, for they exhibit two features: the events recalled are trivial but they are recollected in every detail. In a way which is very much in accord with the rest of his theory of the unconscious, Freud argues that such memories or rather memory traces have a content which offers a point of contact with fantasy. Just as experiences of *déjà-vu* or the uncanny are caused by the linking of a present image to something repressed, and just as dreams contain both an absurd manifest content (what we recall from them) and a latent content (the wish their content makes possible), so the everydayness of screen memories disguises more significant repressed material which has been displaced (*screen* memories therefore).

Da Vinci's vulture memory, Freud suggests, takes memory traces of being suckled by the mother and transforms them so they may express, among other things, the wish to suck a penis (which is what *coda*, tail, can mean in Italian) and so a desire for the phallic mother (the mother with nothing missing). Consistent with the concept of deferred interpretation, screen memories become charged either because the memory traces contain some repressed fantasy material which is activated later or because the subject's later experience retrospectively renders them effective as fantasy. If the subject actually sees itself as a child in the remembered scenario, this is strong evidence that the original impression has been worked over.

Wordsworth's early memories have in common their ordinariness, though with their rural setting more ordinary then than now. And in fact it helps them become points of identification for the reader that they are often typical boyish and tomboyish activities, not clearly class-specific, happening outdoors and so associated with the natural world. By looking in detail at one I shall suggest what wishes it may enact and so what desire structures the other early memories and the later 'spots of time' into a coherent identity.

In *The Prelude* (XII: 287–335) Wordsworth describes coming home from school for Christmas holidays at the age of about 13. He recalls straining his eyes through the mist in anxious expectation for the horses that would bring his brothers and himself home:

> 't was a day
> Tempestuous, dark and wild, and on the grass
> I sate half-sheltered by a naked wall;
> Upon my right hand couched a single sheep,
> Upon my left a blasted hawthorn stood . . .

But within ten days, before they went back to school, his father died. He feels the event was a 'chastisement' for his irritable impatience when waiting for the horses:

> I bowed low
> To God, Who thus corrected my desires;
> And afterwards, the wind and sleety rain,
> And all the business of the elements,
> The single sheep, and the one blasted tree,
> And the bleak music from that old stone wall,
> The noise of wood and water, and the mist
> That on the line of each of those two roads
> Advanced in such indisputable shapes;
> All these were kindred spectacles and sounds
> To which I oft repaired, and thence would drink,
> As at a fountain; and on winter nights,
> Down to this very time, when storm and rain
> Beat on my roof, or, haply, at noon-day,
> While in a grove I walk, whose lofty trees,
> Laden with summer's thickest foliage, rock
> In a strong wind, some working of the spirit,
> Some inward agitations thence are brought,
> Whate'er their office, whether to beguile
> Thoughts over busy in the course they took,
> Or animate an hour of vacant ease.

It is a much-discussed passage, though discussion has tended to concentrate on the content of what is said rather than how it is said. The
overt meaning of this early memory is obvious enough: the young
Wordsworth waited impatiently to get home for the holidays but found
afterwards that his hope was disappointed by the death of his father,
and so learned that you can't always get what you want, God correcting
his desires.

No man, Freud remarks sardonically, feels only grief when his father
dies. An excess in Wordsworth's feelings of guilt ('I bowed low') evinces
the hidden cause for that excess; a part of Wordsworth feels antagonism
towards his father, his 'anxiety of hope' was in part a wish for his father's
death. What happens offsets and contains this motif. As in 'Frost at
Midnight' we have a memory inside a memory; now (in Book XIII)
Wordsworth remembers that time and how then, afterwards, he remembered the wind, the wall, the single sheep, the tree, the mist which he
saw before his father's death. Before they seemed bleak, imparting a
sense of abandonment, isolation and loss, but afterwards they merge
with the mist and with the viewpoint of the observer to become 'kindred
spectacles', offering a sense of unity between object and subject. It is at
this point we may usefully recollect that Freud's account of derealization
relates it not only to defence of the ego but also to 'a child's criticism
of his father'.

How the passage unfolds takes place around a dialectic which might
be summed up as follows. Insofar as subject/object union is a dyadic
relation it pulls the boy into narcissistic confirmation of his own self-
identity and towards incestuous perpetuation of the mother/infant bond;
insofar as subject/object separation implies a breaking of that dyad by
the intervention of a third term, it represents law, the Name of the
Father, and the fact the identity is only borrowed from the Other.
Typically in Wordsworth the movement pulls us from the second to
the first, not just at the level of what is said but, crucially, in terms of
how it is said.

The passage progresses from loss into Oedipal aggression and on into
something different from either, as the death of the father and any wish
for that is framed and contained by the dreariness of the scene and the
visionary dreariness of it as it is remembered. Derealization and the
ensuing sense of dyadic unity replaces any pain or loss engendered by
the father – the content of that memory is subsumed and overridden
by the fact of remembering the moor and the I united:

> All these were kindred spectacles and sounds
> To which I often repaired, and thence would drink,
> As at a fountain.

While what is said refers to loss, the phallus and the father, the way it is said is presided over rather by union, the breast and the mother.

Fathers and mothers

With deliberate provocation William Empson in 1930 wrote that 'Wordsworth frankly had no inspiration other than his use, when a boy, of the mountains as a totem or father-substitute'. That would fit many of the experiences Wordsworth records. After filching game from someone else's snare the young Wordsworth fantasizes:

> Low breathings coming after me, and sounds
> of undistinguishable motion, steps
> Almost as silent as the turf they trod . . .
> (I: 323–5)

Later, he steals a boat, and, as he rows away from the shore 'a huge peak, black and huge' seems to loom over him (previously it had been hidden by a lower summit in the foreground); like Jack the Giant-killer after he has taken the Giant's goose, he is pursued in his imagination by 'huge and mighty forms, that do not live / Like living men,' and these become 'a trouble' to his dreams (I: 398–400). Pre-eminent among these bad memories, there is the murderer's name carved in the turf (XII 223 ff.). Now, all of these imply a guilt which corresponds to the Oedipal transgression they express and would tend to justify Empson's remark.

For explicable meteorological reasons, lush valleys intersect the bleak tops of the Cumbrian landscape, this is recorded in Wordsworth's poetry, and so, adopting Empson's perspective, one might as easily speak of Wordsworth's use, when a boy, of streams and valleys as a mother-substitute. Beginning from the lines which describe how he heard the River Derwent,

> winding among grassy holms
> Where I was looking on, a babe in arms,
> Make ceaseless music . . .
> (I: 275–7)

innumerable passages evoke mist, water, greenery, vales and hollows. And many of those sequences which end up with narratives of paternal aggression begin with images of maternal comfort. 'Fostered alike by beauty and by fear' (I: 302) Wordsworth finds both a mother and a father for himself in his experiences of the natural world.

What makes this effect so striking is that it follows from the effacement of Wordsworth's father and mother from the poem. His father appears finally – already dead – in Book XII. His mother is alluded to, indirectly, when Book II speaks of how 'Blest the infant Babe' is when 'Nursed in his Mother's arms' (II: 232, 235) but the empathic notion of how he 'held mute dialogues with my Mother's heart' (II: 268) introduces a veiled reference to her death (II: 277–81). She hardly figures at all until, entirely out of chronology, her death is mentioned retrospectively in the banal, formal and awkwardly inverted statement that 'Early died / My honoured Mother' (V: 256–7).

Perhaps this vague generalizing of the parents is a literary trope to help us identify with the speaker. Yet it contrasts markedly with the early memories of parents in other writers. Rousseau remembers his father beating his older brother and elsewhere William Wordsworth records similar memories. In his 'Autobiographical Memoranda' dictated a few years before his death, he recalls how his mother died from catching a cold, as well as this little narrative:

> I remember my mother only in some few situations, one of which was her pinning a nosegay to my breast when I was going to say the catechism in the church, as was customary before Easter.

This is another screen memory, and the gift the boy recalls or imagines being given by the mother would be extremely suggestive in a psycho-biography of William Wordsworth. In the narrative presented in *The Prelude* there is nothing remotely like this vivid and detailed incident.

Instead, the mother and her death is spoken of like this:

> I was left alone
> Seeking the visible world, nor knowing why.
> The props of my affections were removed,
> And yet the building stood, as if sustained
> By its own spirit!
> *(II: 277–81)*

Precisely. For what is recorded as fact stands as a wish, the wish that the self might sustain itself in entire independence, without parental origin at all, omnipotent like God in Milton.

The wish that the boy of Winander should be lured by Nature rather than the other way round has strongly incestuous undertones. So does the story in which Wordsworth risks death climbing rocks to rob nests (moving 'as plunderers where the mother-bird' had built her home; I: 327). And phallic sexuality certainly rears its head when he steals a boat and rows out into the middle:

lustily
I dipped my oars into the silent lake,
And, as I rose upon the stroke, my boat,
Went heaving through the water like a swan . . .

(*I: 373–6*)

Yet overall the poem exhibits a remarkable attenuation of sexual drive altogether (a topic to be picked up in Chapter 6). This tends strongly to confirm the psychoanalytic principle that narcissism can redirect sexual desire to non-sexual ends. Or, to put the same point another way: what Wordsworth really desires is himself, standing alone (in more fully Lacanian terms, he desires to retreat from desire into demand). He wants the castle of the self to be sustained 'By its own spirit!', in the words of Shakespeare's Coriolanus:

As if a man were author of himself
And knew no other kin.

(*Act V, scene iii*)

Wordsworth desires to be – in every sense – a self-made man. *The Prelude* is founded in an identical gesture to that caught in Hamm's satiric perspective when he proclaims, proudly and full of self-afflatus, 'But for me no father. But for Hamm no home'.

The condition for this effect is derealization. Discarding the options of representing the Other by animal, childish or adult human figures, *The Prelude* chooses to render it as landscape. Paternal and maternal figures, and the possibilities that go with them, can then be displaced into images of the natural world, objects already half-effaced into subjectivity. Far from being merely a formal effect, an attractive trope or apt vehicle to press feelings, reading meanings into landscape is a necessary condition for what is asserted. In dreams 'landscapes', Freud proposes, 'are invariably the genitals of the dreamer's mother'. In *The Prelude* any idea signifying lack, law, the Name of the Father, and the notion that identity is only borrowed from the Other, is given another, separate meaning by being expressed in a mode consistent with images of the mother's body. The death of the father, for example, is framed and presented as an experience in relation to the natural world and felt to be appropriately symbolized by objects from a landscape. By such means *The Prelude* seeks to ensure that Wordsworth should be wholly himself.

Slogging through all the other 'spots of time' (however these are counted) would still not demonstrate finally that all these 'memorials' were structured by a single principle of order embodying the narcissistic desire as I have outlined it. Each epiphany – his early memories, feeling at university that he was 'not for that hour', the moment of conviction that he was a 'dedicated Spirit', the dream of the Arab and Quixote, and so on down to getting rid of his false *persona* and discovering his 'true self' – all are different. Each one that is added, though meant to reveal, explain and consolidate, in fact slightly alters all the others, the very fact of another instance causing us to revise our perception of any order holding them together. Enough has been said, I hope, to suggest how *The Prelude* supports its claim that there is a true self inhering in the continuity of memories which are coherent, not disparate, necessary, not just accidental. We may now turn to the principle of rhetoric by which that effect of inner necessity is upheld.

5

Autobiography 2: Rhetoric

Hysterics suffer mainly from reminiscences
Breuer and Freud
Studies on Hysteria

Early in 'The Glenn Miller Story' (1954), Miller (James Stewart) tells his wife (June Allyson) that he can hear this sound in his head but just can't quite get the band to play it, and we in the audience all know, as surely as readers of the *Aeneid* would know Aeneas did found Rome, that Miller will get the band to play the sound in his head. Public libraries today each have a large section of biography and autobiography full of texts which follow the narrative convention of the contemporary 'story of my life': after an origin (parentage, birth, schooling), early experiences of failure conceal intimations of future success realized in a latter half as hero or heroine achieves public recognition. When Bob Geldof in the bestselling autobiography of our times, *Is That It?*, mentions his precocious ability at the age of about nine years to memorize 'the lyrics of every song Cliff Richard ever recorded' the reader is encouraged to dismiss the random material in the surrounding context and beam in on Geldof's sense of vocation, confirmed when he founds the Boomtown Rats ('I had found what I was born to do'), a truth the reader already knew anyway when they bought the book. Buried inside *Is That It?* I think we'll find Wordsworth's *Prelude*.

Contingency and necessity

Autobiography is a very complicated effect and I'll try to put forward my understanding of it as briefly and clearly as I can (these are deep waters).

For autobiography summons into play a number of diverse features: an opposition between contingency and necessity (the random material of Geldof's life versus his sense of vocation); narrative; a special conception of temporality; and, since autobiography is always the utterance of an individual, a mode of address which Jacques Lacan analyses as 'full speech'. At stake in autobiography is the condition of personal identity.

A preliminary example of the autobiographical effect, from the popular culture we breathe today, without noticing, as fish do water. During three months of the autumn of 1991 in England the number one love song had a refrain, 'Everything I do, I do for you'. What, everything? Including that? And even *that*? The claim is that every thought and action expresses a personal self (in this case devoted to another), an essence maintained by excluding or marginalizing what counts as accidental. Stephen Gill remarks that Wordsworth has 'a conviction which is repeated in various forms in all his autobiographical poems, namely, that his development obeys a providential economy of loss and gain'. The I of this popular song similarly presents his personal identity as a consequence of necessity, of unspoken destiny.

Thematically, Wordsworth's narrative constructs an opposition between necessity and contingency and equates it with real/apparent and with natural/social. If its immediate poetic model, *Paradise Lost*, turns around the *felix culpa* (fortunate fall) in which God's foresight assures that Adam and Eve will be morally better for eating the apple, then correspondingly *The Prelude* reveals a Wordsworth whose true inward self is better assured by his digression through a false political identity. And this is done, as has been noted already, by founding the poem in the opposition epitomized as the shell and the stone. Further, the promotion of the natural over the social is also performed, in a different mode, in the way Wordsworth's parents as actual social beings get relegated from the scenario in favour of derealized images from Nature. These thematic oppositions, leading to the narrated conclusion of *The Prelude* (that Wordsworth has found his true self) are sustained and confirmed throughout by an autobiographical rhetoric.

At an initial level such rhetoric decides from line to line what details go into and what are kept out of the story. As mentioned already, *The Prelude* is not the only account of his life William Wordsworth wrote. His 'Autobiographical Memoranda' begin like this:

> I was born in Cokermouth, in Cumberland, on April 7th, 1770, the second son of John Wordsworth, attorney-at-law, as lawyers to this class were then called, and law-agent to Sir James Lowther . . . The time of my infancy and early boyhood was passed partly at Cockermouth, and partly with my mother's parents at Penrith, where my mother,

in the year 1778, died of a decline, brought on by a cold, the consequence of being put, at a friend's house in London, in what used to be
called 'a best bedroom'.

Much closer to the traditional 'life and times' story about an individual,
this other narrative is social and quotidian. It is able to include a strong
sense of contingency, the death of the mother because she happened
to stay in an unused bedroom, and this would disqualify the event from
featuring in the poetic autobiography. In the fuller autobiography the
line between what counts as destiny and what as chance is much more
firmly policed. That process of surveillance can be seen very much at
work in Book VII of *The Prelude* when Wordsworth is in London.

London resists Wordsworth's autobiographical narrativization. It is
simply too full

> Of trivial objects, melted and reduced
> To one identity, by differences
> That have no law, no meaning and no end.
>
> (*VII: 726–8*)

for any of it (except the isolated figure of the blind beggar, VII: 638–49)
to be integrated into the substantial self. In a recurrent trope
Wordsworth says of his metropolitan experiences 'I glance but at a few
conspicuous marks . . .' (VII: 574) or 'One will I select . . .' (VII: 602)
or 'From these sights / Take one . . .' (VII: 675–6): as the act of selec-
tions becomes overt, the connotation of necessity gets undermined.
Associated with contingency and false appearance, London must appear
in the poem but has to be denied any value.

Providential narrative

Nobody is born able to tell stories. Competence in narrative, including
a narrative about one's own life that makes a sense of personal identity
possible, is learned, internalized from other people. In autobiographical
discourse discrimination between the contingent and the necessary is
governed by narrative. For narrative (narrating) operates with a double
function. At every point along the way it sorts out what incidents,
feelings and ideas are kept in *and* links together those that are one according to some conception of cause and effect. Just as in history-writing
narrative changes a chronicle into history proper (as we now understand
it), so narrative turns a diary into autobiography. Here is Dorothy
Wordsworth's journal account of a day in the life of herself and William,
27 March 1802, a day on which he (almost certainly) wrote down the

first four stanzas of 'Ode: Intimations of Immortality from Recollections of Early Childhood':

> *Saturday*. A divine morning. At Breakfast Wm wrote part of an ode. Mr Olliff sent the dung and Wm went to work in the garden. We sate all day in the orchard.

Mr Olliff and his gift are too factitious to figure in *The Prelude*, as for that matter is sitting in the garden. Out of the innumerable large and small experiences anyone has even in a short period (a day, a week) autobiography privileges certain ones. It takes the all but inconsequential listing of events as they might appear in a daily diary and transforms them into a coherent order.

To be human is to be able to tell stories and to be an individual means being able to recount some narrative about oneself. Simply the act of narration, as it grows beyond a listing like Dorothy's, accords a sense of meaning and order to what it recalls and records. But *The Prelude*, while acknowledging the effect, wants to affirm something much grander at work than the operation of narrative:

> Dust as we are, the immortal spirit grows
> Like harmony in music; there is a dark
> Inscrutable workmanship that reconciles
> Discordant elements, makes them cling together
> In one society. How strange, that all
> Terrors, pains, and early miseries,
> Regrets, vexations, lassitudes interfused
> Within my mind, should e'er have borne a part,
> And that a needful part, in making up
> The calm existence that is mine when I
> Am worthy of myself!
>
> (I: 340–50)

Here indeed is a 'providential economy', for even the bad times are good, even apparently unnecessary feelings can be revised and recuperated into a 'needful' unity. Despite its official commitment to secular humanism *The Prelude* mystifies the ordering inherent in autobiographical narrative by naming it in supernatural vocabulary – a sense of the spirit as 'immortal' ensues from 'Inscrutable workmanship' (is this God's or the narrator's?). What *is* mysterious or, rather, contradictory in this crafting, workmanship or effect, has to be the notion of temporality on which it depends. For it assumes a temporality in which (1) I can find narrative concatenation *afterwards* through revising, rewriting and re-inscribing what happened at the time, (2) that concatenation stretches from my past prospectively into my future; (3) but both past and future somehow exclude what is happening now, the present moment in which I'm doing all this.

Providential is again exactly the right word for this impossible temporal strategy. Something is providential (Latin: *provideo*, 'I see at a distance') because seen prospectively it had to happen yet I only know it had to happen afterwards, in hindsight. The providential, then, is what Freud speaks of in relation to screen memories by saying that 'we seek in our memories to ascertain what were the impressions that were destined to influence us to the end of our lives'. This is just what *The Prelude* tries to do and accurately describes in terms of an 'inscrutable workmanship'. According to a providential temporality I *seek* for my future in my memories by finding a narrative for them. And that narrativizing confers identity on me.

Narrativizing identity begins with the sentence, for in making sense of a string of signifiers I find a stability for myself. In the process of reading a sentence, as each word arrives, I extrapolate prospectively what it may mean and then retrospectively re-read the sentence when something else arrives to close down its meaning with an anchoring point (by then, of course, I am already wondering what comes next). The process is structured in the same way as deferred interpretation in a subject, who both fantasises prospectively what his or her life will mean and retrospectively re-interprets memories whenever something happens that seems to hold the thing together. Interaction of memory and fantasy entails that the subject never simply is ('I am'): the little scenes from the past, the memory traces, are always rewritten by the present act of remembering because they get caught up in fantasies projected into the future. I can only think about who I was by imagining what I would like to be – far from being fixed and present, my identity, therefore, is not what I am but what *I will have been*. Consequently, as Hamm says in *Endgame*, 'I was never there'.

But wait a minute, *who* says 'I was never there'? Stability is accorded to self-identity to the degree that what is happening now can be excluded from the narrative, that is, the act of narrativizing. But this fixity can never be more than provisional (Wordsworth wants it to be absolute) because utterance, whether spoken or written, always takes place in what Emile Benveniste speaks of as 'the unceasing present of enunciation'. In this respect the autobiographical effect is always dependent on a present moment and on an act of speech or confession.

Full speech and empty speech

In contemporary Western society we confess all the time. People accused of crimes confess to the police, patients tell doctors their symptoms, students explain to teachers why essays are late, children admit to parents why they really want something, lovers bare their souls to each other, in psychoanalytic therapy the analyst tries to work out with the analysand the truth about his or her life, and Wordsworth in *The Prelude* talks to Coleridge about the growth of his mind. While remembering, trying to tell the truth about oneself in the form of a narrative, the I cannot but lay claim to a sense of imaginary coherence. Precisely the kind of confessional discourse the analyst listens to from the analysand, Jacques Lacan refers to this as 'full speech' and defines it by saying its effect (workmanship) 'is to reorder past contingencies by conferring on them the sense of necessities to come'.

The struggle to give voice to full speech, the impossible but inescapable attempt to say who I really am – now – depends upon and has as its condition what Lacan calls 'empty speech': 'For in this labour (i.e. talking to the analyst) which he undertakes to reconstruct *for another*, he rediscovers the fundamental alienation that made him construct it *like another*, and which has always destined it to be taken from him *by another*'. That is, in trying to confess:

1 I have to address myself to someone else so that my awareness of them and who they are gets inside my speech, shaping what I say.
2 I can only speak in a shared discourse so that nothing I say, if it is to be intelligible, could not in principle be said by someone else (there is no private language).
3 I may think I am speaking exclusively to and for my addressee but it follows from (2) that my words could be understood by anyone.

Empty speech means, as Beckett's the Unnameable says, 'I'm in words, made of words, others' words', and it is this insistence of the Other at the heart of my sincere attempt to talk for and about myself which renders my full speech necessary only if I can confiscate the emptiness of speech which makes it possible. But of course I can't – I can only be myself by disavowing and denying what prevents me ever being only myself.

Refusing to concede that identity is a position, a temporary coherence, *The Prelude* tries to promote Wordsworth's identity as self-sufficient and complete by transforming accident into essence, difference into sameness, contingency into destiny. As a condition for this plenitude, it must shut down empty speech, speech that is for another, like another's and taken up by another. Wordsworth envisions himself as speaking to

Coleridge, the 'Dear Friend' always imagined as present and frequently addressed. In doing so he seeks to find himself perfectly reflected in his addressee, a kindred soul, in the spirit in which he writes of the 'Immortality' Ode, 'A Reader who has not a vivid recollection of these feelings having existed in his mind cannot understand that poem'. And, as will be explored in more detail in the chapter on language still to come, Wordsworth also tries to make his speech pertain only to himself and express only himself. But, however hard the Wordsworth of the text strained to enclose himself hermetically in a full speech *then*, his intelligibility depends on a discourse available to us *now*, so that – as this present book itself evidences – if we can understand him at all, he is to that extent taken away from himself, his project is undone.

The I now and then

Unlike words, photographs resemble, iconically, what they refer to. The more alive the people in them seem, the more dead we know they are; the more vividly present, the more actually absent. That sad smile of John Lennon as a boy on my cover is so graphic he could be alive now if the fact of the photograph itself did not presage his death, his absence, along with the 1940s which gave him that cow's lick haircut, the V-neck pullover and his smile.

Suppose someone is looking at a shot of themselves when they were much younger, then the same balance of gain and loss is increased on both sides. Suppose now William Wordsworth once walked eight and a half miles inland from Duddon Sands along the valley of the River Lickle and up across Brown Pike to the top of the Old Man of Coniston (2631 ft), and then, if it was a clear day, looked back in a south-westerly direction at where he had come from. He would see something like what is described in stanza IX of the 'Immortality' Ode:

> Hence in a season of calm weather
> Though inland far we be,
> Our Souls have sight of that immortal sea
> Which brought us hither,
> Can in a moment travel thither,
> And see the Children sport upon the shore,
> And hear the mighty waters rolling evermore.

What we have is a helicopter shot as the camera zooms in on the children and (this implied but not stated) I suddenly see one of the children playing on the sand is me. On this evidence it's clear that Wordsworth's impossible, narcissistic object of desire is himself or rather to see himself or rather to see himself seeing himself.

There is a strategy, then, in terms of vision. The early memories in *The Prelude* – skating, snaring birds, the name of the murderer in the grass, the death of the father – each of these is like a photograph of the young Wordsworth, an idealized picture to be sure, since it shows a Wordsworth less self-conscious, more deeply immersed in the dyadic union between subject and object, closer to the mother, more immune to difference. This is Wordsworth as he would like to see himself but of course no longer can. Though the absence or loss or lack the image reminds him of can never really be made good, perhaps it can be made good if this image is treated as an object in which the subject can imagine himself reflected, a mirror in which he sees himself. An analysis of *The Prelude* along these lines has been well followed through by Robert Young, who demonstrates how it 'winds its way from one moment of assuagement of lack to another, questing in a quest that can never be realised'. Wordsworth's desire is to reify 'something ever more about to be' into an object, a 'glory' he can 'recognise' and say he recognizes (VI: 608, 605).

And there is a strategy in terms of speech and writing. Wordsworth wants to talk about himself, say what he's really like. But just as the face in the mirror is not the same as the face of the person looking at the mirror (one face is represented in the mirror, the other is looking at it from somewhere else), so the I spoken about, represented in discourse, is not identical with the subject who is actually doing the talking or reading the writing in the present. Once again, on the grounds of language, the absence of the real self is reinstated and once again there is a protracted effort to make it good, to make the memory (in which Wordsworth is himself) come alive again while it is actually being talked about in the present (so he can see himself). In the 'Preface' to *Lyrical Ballads* the strategy is described in terms of an original emotion and the attempt to reproduce it in the present for an act of poetic composition:

> I have said that poetry is the spontaneous overflow of powerful feelings; it takes its origin from emotion recollected in tranquillity: the emotion is contemplated till, by a species of re-action, the tranquillity gradually disappears, and an emotion, kindred to that which was before the subject of contemplation, is gradually produced, and does itself actually exist in the mind. In this mood successful composition generally begins, and in a mood similar to this it is carried on . . .

But the emotion in the present is indeed in the present and though it may be 'kindred' to what was in the past, it is not and never can be the same as that. A gap remains which a special deployment of language tries to repair.

At one point *The Prelude* suggests that the difference between the Wordsworth speaking now and the Wordsworth then, in his memories, is so great it is as though he were two people:

> so wide appears
> The vacancy between me and those days
> Which yet have such self-presence in my mind,
> That, musing on them, often do I seem
> Two consciousnesses, conscious of myself
> And of some other being.
>
> (*II: 28–33*)

Is Wordsworth giving it all away here, leaving it only to open for a reader to reply that this 'do seem' is an 'is', that there are two consciousnesses, one past, one present, which can never be the same? To argue that would be to underestimate the complex subtlety – the modernity – of the poem and its ways of trying to make good this split. In the passage I cited earlier to instance the providential nature of full speech, all kinds of losses being a 'needful part' of identity (I: 340–50), Wordsworth mentions 'Regrets'. He is not the only one to have them.

To say 'I did it my way' is another way to claim my identity is destiny. When Frank Sinatra famously sings that as for regrets, he's 'had a few' but then again 'too few to mention' there is surely some troubling disturbance in the text. Has he had regrets or not? If you regret what you haven't got, how do you 'have' a regret? And even in saying they were too few to mention, surely he is actually mentioning them? Common sense rushes to our aid here because obviously he must mean that they were hardly worth mentioning or only just worth mentioning. But this isn't what the words say, an Oxford philosopher or even a strict literary critic might soon reply. In fact two I's or selves must be in play here: one the I represented in the text who has indeed had so few regrets they are not worth mentioning, and another I, the speaker (or singer) of the text, who does have regrets and does mention them. The position on these two I's is even clearer when someone says, 'I can't think of anything to say', representing themselves in the words as being at a loss but by the very fact of speaking the words finding something to say. Linguistics terms the represented self and the speaking self 'the subject of the enounced' (or statement) and the 'subject of enunciation' (or utterance) respectively though the terminology matters less than the effect. For in Wordsworth it occurs all the time, as was noted first in the case of 'My heart leaps up'.

This play or doubling of the self is always inherent in the question of regrets. Is a regret there or not? Present or absent? Pace Frank Sinatra, you don't only regret missed opportunities but all the ones you've taken as well. For, like the loved ones in old photographs, all the experiences you've had are absent, missing, past, lost except for the memory traces in which you recall them now. So experiences are always regretted. When Edith Piaf sings, 'Non, je ne regrette rien' ('No, I regret nothing') one self claims it regrets nothing while another, by the act of denying regret, admits that it might. More honest is Samuel Beckett's character, Watt, who (in contrast to the fulsomely expressive Edith) exclaims:

> Personally of course I regret everything. Not a word, not a deed, not a thought, not a need, not a grief, not a joy, not a girl, not a boy, not a doubt, not a trust, not a scorn, not a lust, not a hope, not a fear, not a smile, not a tear, not a name, not a face, no time, no place, that I do not regret, exceedingly.

(Lest this should encourage too sympathetic a view of Watt, I have to record that his next sentence is, 'An ordure, from beginning to end'.) Wordsworth's poetry uses these two consciousnesses, the split between the I represented and the I that does the speaking, to effect a recuperation of loss. When he writes, 'Regretted – that word, too, was on my tongue' (IV: 132), he refers to what he says ('Regretted!') almost as though the one who speaks it is someone else, and he amplifies the notion of regret and loss with a strangely cumbersome metaphor which makes the idea and the word sound as though they were present, situated 'on my tongue'.

Recuperating loss 1

Back in his book, *Mythologies*, written in the early 1950s, Roland Barthes analysed the process of recuperation in terms of what he called 'Operation Margarine'. An advertisement admits that a substance is margarine in the context of saying it tastes nearly as good as butter and is cheaper too – so it's better *after all*. That figure of 'in the end' or 'after all' exemplifies recuperation; minor flaws are conceded (some police are bad apples) – represented in fact as only accidental defects – so that the wider order may be justified (the system, like the barrel of apples as a whole, is alright after all).

Taking back by giving something away is a function subjectivity can readily perform, especially if we recall that for psychoanalysis there are always three agencies at work in any individual, the id, the ego and the superego. Briefly, melancholia may result from the death of a loved one. The lost object may be kept as though alive if its place is taken by the I through 'an *identification* of the ego with the abandoned object'. But this only happens on condition the superego becomes active in criticizing and judging the ego from a position of some detachment from it (in the classic example, Hamlet's bitter self-reproaches for insufficiently mourning his father serve to keep his father's memory present to him).

On this model we can understand self-pity, that particularly pleasurable emotion of 'feeling sorry for yourself'. Evidently, there are two selves at stake when melancholia operates in this way. One, the I, is admitted to be suffering loss or to be like a lost object but this admission is facilitated because there is another, more superior I who stands as it were apart from and outside the first I. Employing this strategy you can amass a virtual universe of lost objects, kept because you know they are lost. You can in fact find a special pleasure in regretting everything – it may even be, as Lacan suggests, that you may be the process of that regret.

That this structure of melancholy regret or self-pity has a relevance to Wordsworth's poetry can hardly be missed, for it maps onto and coincides with the split between the represented self and the speaking self. When approaching this issue, however, it is absolutely essential to resist the blandishments of conventional literary criticism and keep steadfastly in mind the fact that William Wordsworth is dead – utterly dead – and not available to speak the poetry published in his name at any price, nor has been since 1850, and that the only person who speaks or reads or performs the lines is us now, readers in the present. We are the only ones who can occupy the position of speaking subject and so for us any I who figures in the text is only a represented I, precisely the I of the poem.

Just as there is a split between the remembered or lost self and the critical self who would resurrect that self by mourning it, so there is a disjunction between a represented I who is lost or has regrets and the further position of the speaking subject who is not lost and does not regret. Through this disjunction even a negation can become a means of assertion and I can have regrets while saying I don't. In the 'Tintern Abbey' poem the speaker's admission of failure within the text – 'I cannot paint / What then I was' – is compensated for by the reader's sense that the poem has demonstrated the past in a vivid recreation. Or again when the I of the poem mourns his loss, on one occasion with the words, 'If this / Be but a vain belief . . .', later with

> Nor perchance,
> If I were not thus taught, should I the more
> Suffer my genial spirits to decay ...

the reader reproducing the poem in the present and so at some remove from the I which seems to despair, is invited to feel reassured that the rest of the text shows it was not a vain belief, that the speaker is taught, that his genial spirits are not decaying. Such confidence arises because the reader can master the represented speaker's misery from a superior position.

The trope of regret or pathos is used all over *The Prelude*, though a key instance occurs in Book XII. The Wordsworth in the text says:

> I am lost, but see
> In simple childhood something of base
> On which thy greatness stands ...
> *(XII: 273–5)*

and goes on to describe his loss – and increasing loss – of the past. How can this strike the reader, who is free at any point to flip the pages back to Book I and re-read the great memorials set up there, the reader for whom the narrative of *The Prelude*, not only early memories but Cambridge, London, the French Revolution, the speaker's despair and recovery, all this is laid out and made available to him or her in a position the Wordsworth represented in the text at this point can never occupy? The words which name the regret are there both for the represented I and for the reader but each takes them differently. The I in the poem who says he is lost is not the same I as that of the reader who reads these words.

There is a complication here I would really prefer to dodge. A representation of the split between represented speaker and speaking subject is *itself* introduced into the poem. From what I've argued so far it would seem as if *The Prelude* consisted mainly of a linear narrative of past memories interleaved with attempts to bring those memories alive in the present. It does not, for it actually consists of something much more like a spoken stream of consciousness. The poem presents itself as a protracted speech, and it is consistent with this that William Wordsworth did recite it to Coleridge on 'successive evenings' around Christmas 1806. And the poem shows Wordsworth constantly manoeuvring between apologies:

> My drift I fear
> Is scarcely obvious ...
> *(V: 293–4)*

justifications:

> Ah! need I say, dear Friend! that to the brim
> My heart was full . . .
>
> *(IV: 332–3)*

explanations:

> Points have we all of us within our souls . . .
>
> *(III: 188)*

repetitions:

> the fault
> This I repeat, was mine . . .
> *(VI: 188–9)*

professions of total honesty:

> . . . with my best conjecture I would trace
> Our Being's earthly progress . . .
>
> *(II: 234–5)*

doubts about his own motives:

> not misled, I trust,
> By an infirmity of love for days
> Disowned by memory . . .
> *(I: 13–15)*

and so on and so on (it is this voice which first-time readers of the poem generally find so off-putting, and not only them). As well as recorded *memories*, present re-livings or *recreations* of past experience, there is another level which resolves itself into *reflections* of this kind.

A well-known example is the crossing of the Alps in Book VI. Wordsworth and his companion, in anxious anticipation of crossing the Alps, find out from a peasant that they have missed the road, crossed the Alps without knowing it, so must go back – so much is memory recorded in the narrative (VI: 557–591). They go down to the right road and Wordsworth is overwhelmed by the sight:

> The immeasurable height
> Of woods decaying, never to be decayed,
> The stationary blasts of waterfalls,
> And in the narrow rent at every turn
> Winds thwarting winds, bewildered and forlorn . . .
> *(VI: 624–8)*

Urgent rhythms carry the reader forward across a list of separate items in parallel ('The torrents', 'The rocks', 'the raving stream') by means of a developed syntax reaching its climax in rapt, prophetic, Biblical vocabulary and diction:

> Characters of the Great Apocalypse,
> The types and symbols of Eternity,
> Of first, and last, and midst, and without end.
>
> (*VI: 638–40*)

The tone of voice here is a firm token that the memory is being recollected, relived now, as a present fantasy. However, woven in between this and the straight narrative there is a passage of reflection on the autonomous power of 'Imagination, (VI: 592–616), its capacity to act in some independence from perception of the natural world.

This level of reflection, which actually makes up half the poem, expresses a form of rational self-awareness. Such self-consciousness attempts to provide a meaning for being, to understand and interpret. Wordsworth's would-be full speech does not merely seek to integrate a past into a present self but also to become aware of and recognize the destiny thus achieved. So *The Prelude* confidently advances an interpretation of Wordsworth's life and something of human life as well, very much what was surveyed and criticized here in Chapter 2. The Wordsworth speaking to us now is assured that in retrospect he can know and master his past life, especially by imposing that opposition so crucial to any process of knowledge, the distinction between true and false. If London and the failure of his rational hopes in the Revolution prove to be – have been – an untrustworthy appearance, then the continuity between his earlier memories from before the great crisis and new life now can be defended as essential and real. In the metaphor of the poem, the crisis is simply a road over which the stream of his 'true self' flowed in a single, uninterrupted identity (XI: 337–42). In this way he can know himself.

The effect, then, is not simply that Wordsworth has an idealized past self in which he hopes to see himself reflected in the present. A further twist endeavours to double the subject/object relation. In a first level his past self becomes a perfect object for whom present self may be the subject, but in a second that process itself becomes a form of object in which the present reflecting subject may know himself. While the first level has the advantages of being, the second seeks to add to these the benefit of meaning – Wordsworth's attempt is for him to see himself seeing himself.

As one might predict, there are problems with this strategy. One is that temporally or diachronically the autobiographical project is negated by the problem of fixing a moment in time at which the story can be told

and understood. In fact, an overlapping series of Wordsworths is represented within *The Prelude* – Wordsworth as baby, as boy, as adolescent,
at university, visiting France for the first time, in London, living in
France, disillusioned with the French Revolution, apparently restored
to himself, apparently mature at last. Written from the point of view
and interpretative stance of where he is now, the poem claims to be
able to separate true from false selves in retrospect. But if the revolutionary Wordsworth had written his autobiography it would have been
a different narrative with a different interpretation of the past. Each of
this series of selves comes with an interpretative stance attached, trying
to re-transcribe contingent into necessary experience, and this renders
the freezing of the process as it is even in the 1850 published version
just that – a version, not the final truth it would like to claim.

Related to this but not quite the same, there is a discursive difficulty,
ensuing from the disjunction between represented and speaking self, to
name it yet again. Self-reflection – or, rather, the act of self-reflecting –
becomes an attempt to step beyond or outside the previous split. Each
attempt to see himself seeing himself, know himself as he says he is,
tries to close the gap between Wordsworth as he sees himself and
Wordsworth as we see him. Wordsworth inside the poem would really
like to join us outside the poem. Alas, it can't be done. When Alfred
Hitchcock pops up in an Alfred Hitchcock film – carrying a double bass,
wearing a silly hat – that representation of Hitchcock remains inside
the text and an effect of it even if Hitchcock is directing the movie.
If I see a television advertisement which includes a shot of a man
watching a television set on whose screen the same man is shown
watching a screen . . . and so on down to invisibility, the whole series
of screens within screens all remain something represented on my
television set. If Wordsworth says something about himself and then
says something about what he's said and then something about that,
and so on in (potentially) infinite recourse, he still stays inside the text
of *The Prelude*. Wordsworth, even the Wordsworth caught in the very
act of saying to us in such an intimately confiding voice, 'My drift I
fear / Is scarcely obvious', that Wordsworth is an effect of the text, a
textual ghost who can only be raised if we breathe life into him (of which
much more in Chapter 7).

In our own time no-one has written out the impossibility of saying
who you are with more plangent eloquence than Samuel Beckett in his
series of novels, *Murphy, Watt, Molloy, Malone Dies*, culminating in *The
Unnameable*. The unidentified narrator of this text, like the Descartes
of the *Meditations*, wants to identify himself, but on the first page finds,
'I seem to speak, it is not I, about me, it is not about me'. He recognizes

that a previous strategy of trying to identify himself in 'all these Murphys, Molloys, and Malones' – heroes (if that's the word) of Beckett's earlier novels – was a waste of time and that he 'should have spoken of me and me alone':

> It's of me now I must speak, even if I have to do it with their language, it will be a start, a step towards silence and the end of madness, the madness of having to speak and not being able to, except of things that don't concern me, that don't count, that I don't believe, that they have crammed me full of to prevent me saying who I am . . .

But trying to tell his own story instead of theirs is no more of a success because he's in language, made of language; so he begins to invent characters – Basil, Mahood, Worm and others – and tell their stories in the hope that he can slip inside them, that as a speaking subject he can find himself reflected in his objects, these represented identities. Failure again, meaning and being still won't occupy the same space: 'I'm Worm, no, if I were Worm I wouldn't know it, I wouldn't say it, I wouldn't say anything, I'd be Worm'. After this modernist nostalgia for a lost, transcendental self, postmodernist fiction had to forget nostalgia and move on, to somewhere else, leaving us for our present purposes with this question from *The Unnameable*: does any other text show so completely the absurd agony of a self trying to identify itself or provide a more telling commentary on *The Prelude*?

Recuperating loss 2

At the same time this split between the two I's or two subjects for the poem produces another effect and another kind of recuperation. For it enables a displacement from the outside of the poem to its inside, from 'form' into 'content', from the plane of performance to the plane of statement. Just as the metaphor of the police force as a barrel of apples works to transform the idea that a social institution has inherent defects by re-presenting them as the moral rottenness of only too human individuals, so *The Prelude* reconstructs loss by displacing it from the larger world of the poem into the smaller world of what the I in the poem says. Though it is not easy to decide in any situation what depth of mourning would be appropriate, I suggest that the I of *The Prelude* mourns too much (everybody has to grow up sooner or later). This excess is a symptom that a sense of loss arising from sources other than that explicitly admitted by the poem is to be made good by this mourning.

If so, it is not hard to guess what the loss might be. As Catherine Belsey acutely observes, since the full subject, the transcendental I which is its own origin, is impossible, there has been a solid tradition in England associating a rhetoric of pathos with this acknowledgement. It occurs in Locke, for example, and she picks out 'the following elegiac sentence' as typical of the way stated failure is to be restored in the way it is said: 'Tis past controversy, that we have in us something that thinks, our very doubts about what it is, confirm the certainty of its being, though we must content our selves in the ignorance of what kind of being it is'. The poetry of Wordsworth picks up this traditional mode of discourse, intensifies it, enormously magnifies it, and passes it on to us who now find it almost impossible to speak about ourselves without lapsing into this Wordsworthian mode. His mourning is a recuperative mourning for what could never be in the first place, except as an effect: the full subject.

The effect of recuperative displacement once allowed, it's not hard to think of other causes for the grief expressed. In view of the overall argument of *The Prelude* – the transcendental self is the only way to give meaning to human life now that political change has failed – it is tempting to countenance another possible displacement: that the poem represents an act of mourning for a historical loss, the loss dating from Wordsworth's time of any social and collective bond able to confer significance on the life of the individual.

Ode: *Intimations of Immortality*

One poem besides *The Prelude* in particular brings into action most of the themes and effects so far discussed. The 'Immortality' Ode takes the last three lines from 'My heart leaps up' as its epigraph and then enlarges and develops that structure. Its full title is 'Intimations of Immortality from Recollections of Early Childhood' though I shall begin my account by thinking of it as entitled 'Memories of Primary Narcissism and Imaginary Plenitude taken as Guarantees that the I is Self-Sufficient and Not Constituted in Relation to the Other'.

The first four stanzas of the poem perform an act of mourning. Frequently, monosyllabic diction lends the voice the tones of simple declarative statement but this effect of simplicity is offset by a carefully sustained syntax reaching across short two- and three-beat lines to yield the occasional weighty procession of a six-beat line unusual in English:

> There was a time when meadow, grove and stream,
> The earth, and every common sight,
>   To me did seem

> Apparelled in celestial light,
> The glory and the freshness of a dream.
> It is not now as it has been of yore; –
> Turn whereso'er I may,
> By night or day,
> The things which I have seen I now can see no more.

The I is not present in the subject from the first but comes about as a split opens up between the I and the outside world. As Freud writes in a passage quoted by Lionel Trilling in his well-known essay on this poem:

> Originally the ego includes everything, later it detaches from itself the outside world. The ego-feeling we are aware of now is thus only a shrunken vestige of a more extensive feeling – a feeling which embraced the universe and expressed an inseparable connection of the ego with the external world.

That feeling of complete unity between subject and object can be remembered by someone who has passed beyond it – can in fact only by remembered by a subject who has become able to separate its past from its present. As a non-speaking subject the infant inhabits being, a state which can be valued, given meaning, only once the subject has entered discourse and the world of difference. Reversing the notion that we pass forward from the darkness of birth into the daylight of normal life, the 'Immortality' Ode writes of our birth as 'a forgetting' of the oceanic state (Freud's phrase) of primary narcissism and so a passage from light into the 'shades of the prison-house' of everyday life.

After millennia in which life was believed to emerge after birth, it would not be possible to write so challengingly that 'Our birth is but a sleep and a forgetting' without a deliberate irony which acknowledges the opposite position. That irony is made more of in stanza VII, which celebrates the child's transition from being to meaning as the child could not itself celebrate it. In scathing tones the poem speaks of the child as a 'little Actor' learning its role in adult society, 'As if his whole vocation / Were endless imitation'. What is the ironic over-statement effacing here and in the next stanza? If we keep in mind an alternative point of view which affirms that 'the ego has to be developed', that the I comes about in a dialectic in which it wins its identity from the Other, then it becomes plausible to interrogate the opposition the poem assumes but dare not state without ironic cover: that self is inborn and surrenders rather than gains identity in its relation with the Other. What makes the opposition persuasive must be its reliance on something ideological: a perceived nullity in social life ('endless imitation') corresponds to and activates demand for an autonomous self, that absolute notion of self in turn confirming absence of 'real' value in the Other.

Irony ensures that the poem does not mean what it seems to be explicitly saying here and this is how it aims to complete itself successfully. The infant inhabits (is) a unity between subject and object but for that reason doesn't know it but the speaker does because he (it is a he) isn't; he can speak well of infancy only because he can speak at all. The poem treats that contradiction by keeping the reader's awareness of it out of sight, hiding it within ironic exaggeration. It is there nevertheless to be drawn on after the turn at the beginning of stanza IX, 'O joy! that in embers / Is something that doth live . . .'. Since he never really meant it was better to stay a baby, we welcome his admission that it isn't and that in any case we keep our early memories:

> Though nothing can bring back the hour
> Of splendour in the grass, of glory in the flower;
> We will grieve not, rather find
> Strength in what remains behind;
> In the primal sympathy
> Which having been must ever be . . .

There are many different avenues through this particular text. The one I have preferred here, while hoping to catch up and illustrate many of the arguments made in this and the previous chapter, has tended to emphasize the dislocation between the rhetoric of the poem and the content of what the speaker states, that it never means what it says. It would itself be ironic to conclude that the 'Immortality' Ode works (if it does) because of rhetoric, what it actually dismisses as another bit of 'endless imitation'.

In another main aspect the logic and rhetoric of the 'Immortality' Ode are askew. In a central statement the poem declares:

> Our birth is but a sleep and a forgetting:
> The Soul that rises with us, our life's star,
> Hath had elsewhere its setting . . .

Is the self innate and autonomous or is it produced as a culture effect? Christianity is committed to the view that the soul is as Gerard Manley Hopkins wrote, 'an immortal diamond', a view opposed to Wordsworth's secular humanism well epitomized when *The Prelude* refers to this 'very world' of 'all of us' where we must 'find our happiness, or not at all' (XI: 142ff.). It is therefore with a certain hesitancy that William Wordsworth, talking to Isabella Fenwick in 1843, tries to justify the way the 'Immortality' Ode assumes the pre-existence of the soul: 'I took hold of the notion of pre-existence as having sufficient foundation in humanity for authorising me to make for my purpose the best use I could of it as a poet'. But the hesitation is not misplaced, for in assuming the self is innate and autonomous the poem does commit itself to the transcendental origin of the self, despite denegations. Its logic therefore contradicts itself, for an entirely different text would ensue if transcendental pre-existence were followed through: instead of ending elegiacally in acknowledged once-and-for-all, irremediable loss, the poem would end – like *Paradise Lost* – by seeing the fall of the infant subject into human society as fortunate, prelude to the ultimate return – after death – of the soul to 'God, who is our home'.

Why then does the 'Immortality' Ode need to anchor itself to this supernatural rock? Because then in the early nineteenth century, no other grounding could adequately resist acknowledgment that the human self is a cultural effect; because only on this foundation can the text structure itself around a radical and irreconcilable opposition between the value of the self and the valueless fact of social life, 'the prison house'. This gap or fissure in the text exposes the wish on which it founds itself – that the individual should bear within itself an identity transcending any reliance on the Other.

There has never been a human society in which individuals were not able to demarcate their identities from that of other people, to name themselves, to capture for themselves a coherent – and therefore individual – position to speak from within the flux of discourse. In Western Europe, perhaps as early as the 1100s and marked for instance in the poetry of Courtly love, the theory and practice of individuality begins to scoop out for itself an unprecedented dimension of inwardness and velleity. With the Renaissance inner individuality becomes increasingly categorized in an opposition between itself and an outward, social role, so that Lacan, with Descartes in mind, refers to 'this historical moment at the beginning of the seventeenth century' as the 'inaugural moment of the emergence of the subject'. With Romanticism the opposition between self and world tends to become absolute, the I seeking full speech for itself, a personal narrative transforming contingencies into a necessity by re-imagining the traces of memories as a pre-given structure.

As Rousseau writes in the opening sentences of the *Confessions*:

> I have resolved on an enterprise which has no precedent, and which, once complete, will have no imitator. My purpose is to display to my kind a portrait in every way true to nature, and the man I shall portray will be myself. Simply myself. I know my own heart and understand my fellow man. But I am made unlike any one I have ever met; I will even

venture to say that I am like no one in the world. I may be no better, but at least I am different.

Rousseau is imitated by Wordsworth when he claims his text is unprecedented (these rapidly become the conventions of autobiography). How can the autobiographer find a language unique to one person but readable by all? How can the I spoken about ever coincide with the I which is speaking, the I then with the now in which I speak? So, while individual identity is necessary, autobiography is impossible. And we might return to the earlier question of why attempt autobiography, which is also the question, why look for yourself in your personal memories, why the obsession with capturing yourself in a frozen image from the past? *'Hysterics'*, write Breuer and Freud in their *Studies in Hysteria*, *'suffer mainly from reminiscences'*. The hysteric is hysterical because he or she is insecure, uncertain particularly which sex they want to be, and this suggests a link between Romantic autobiography and the earlier chapter on Romantic ideology. In a historical innovation and newly uncertain about its identity, the subject is driven to desire a transcendent self by just what that apparent plenitude would deny. The next chapter will consider how all these themes and effects are played out – with a difference – in the domain of gender.

— 6 ——

Gender

Life it selfe is but Motion, and can never be
without Desire.

Thomas Hobbes

By the end of the seventeenth century in Europe love had become
equated with desire, and sexuality reduced to a bagatelle, though a
game in which women were generally the losers since they were what
was at stake. *Paradise Lost* (1667) treats gender with epic dignity but
after that the situation can be typified by this verse from a song in
Dryden's play, *The Spanish Fryar or, The Double Discovery* (1681) (it is
sung by a woman):

> FARWELL ungratefull Traytor,
>   Farwell my perjur'd Swain,
> Let never injur'd Creature
> Believe a Man again.
> The Pleasure of Possessing
> Surpasses all Expressing,
> But 'tis too short a Blessing,
>   And Love too long a pain.

Romanticism approached gender and sexuality with renewed seriousness,
though it did so at a price, as Thomas Laqueur shows. With Romanticism,
woman begins to lose her anciently established characterization as a
failed man and begins to be seen, in a two-edged development, both in
her difference and as an opposite to be contained by a newly invigorated
masculinity.

   Christine Battersby argues:

> 'I am the author.' 'I am male.' 'I am God.' Romantic and modernist
> art binds these three sentences together into an unholy trinity.

Reintroducing an old idea, Romanticism characterizes the artist as a genius and defines the genius as one who includes both masculine and feminine attributes. While this modifies certain traditional assumptions it does not overthrow them, for the male genius, by incorporating feminine features, actually masters them – when Mick Jagger wore a frock at the Hyde Park concert on 5 June 1969 it affirmed a masculinity so strong it could even contain femininity.

In Godard's 1967 film, 'Weekend', characters keep asking each other, 'Who would you rather sleep with?', naming, say, Stalin and Mao. To pose the option as Wordsworth or Coleridge would show immediately that, in a loose sense, Coleridge is sexy but Wordsworth is not. It is this apparent indifference to sexual desire of any kind which has given Wordsworth his reputation for firm masculinity. Shelley in 'Peter Bell the Third' calls him 'A solemn and unsexual man' (1: 551) and Coleridge, talking about William Wordsworth, confirms this view but phrases it differently by saying that, 'of all the men I ever knew, Wordsworth has the least femininity in his mind'. Virginia Woolf has no doubt what the apparent absence of sexual feeling implies:

> Milton and Ben Jonson had a dash too much of the male in them.
> So had Wordsworth and Tolstoi.

In one respect, these judgements seem a little surprising. Love, the delicious misrecognition that there is a sexual relation (in fact it 'does not take place'), is peculiarly suited to dramatize the necessity of full speech and a would-be mutual recognition between partners, 'I see you as you see me'. Our songs overflow with the idea that 'You are my destiny', that birds gotta fly and fish gotta swim, and so, with a force like that of biological determinism, she must love 'this man of mine' and, reciprocally, he her. With his commitment to the possibility of full speech and completed identity one might expect Wordsworth's heart to leap up at the chance of seeing himself reflected in a lover's eyes. Far from it. As Catherine Belsey argues in a witty and lucid essay, 'the impossible project of Wordsworth's poetry is to hold desire at bay'. Wordsworth's desire is to eradicate desire and to get rid of difference. He wants to be the phallus and have the phallus.

Heterosexual desire

Gayatri Spivak argues that *The Prelude* can only set up the structure it does, will only work, on condition 'Woman [is] shut out'. In France in 1791–92, William Wordsworth and Annette Vallon had an unhappy love affair. Book IX in the 1805 version of *The Prelude* ends with 380 lines, inserted into the residence in France, telling the story of the tragic love affair of Vaudracour and Julia. In *The Prelude* as published in 1850 this story is reduced to 32 lines (IX: 553–85), and, instead of beginning:

> Oh, happy time of youthful lovers, (thus
> My story may begin) . . .

as it does in 1805, in 1850 this has become:

> Oh, happy time of youthful lovers, (thus
> The story might begin) . . .
>
> (*IX: 553–4*)

If you exclude woman, you deny heterosexual desire, you deny paternity and leave a way open for a man to imagine himself as 'son *and* lover, father *and* mother of poems, male *and* female at once', as Spivak says.

No place is provided in the thematic, psychic and tonal economy of *The Prelude* for the expression of male heterosexual desire. Of this the story of Vaudracour and Julia is not the only instance. 'Nutting', a blank verse paragraph describing how a boy alone in the woods gathers some hazel nuts, was written in 1799 and published in the 1800 edition of *Lyrical Ballads*. A seemingly everyday schoolboy adventure becomes very highly charged:

> the hazels rose
> Tall and erect, with tempting clusters hung,
> A virgin scene! – A little while I stood,
> Breathing with such suppression of the heart
> As joy delights in; and, with wise restraint
> Voluptuous, fearless of a rival, eyed
> The banquet . . .
> Then up I rose,
> And dragged to earth both branch and bough, with crash
> And merciless ravage: and the shady nook
> Of hazels, and the green and mossy bower,
> Deformed and sullied, patiently gave up
> Their quiet being . . .

A rape fantasy is distinctly visible beneath the surface of the manifest narrative, though that narrative is there, displacing the feelings into an experience of the natural world and, as usual, into the framing of a dyadic relation (this is Wordsworth, not Byron). Considered for *The Prelude*, the passage was rightly excised for being simply too erotic for that text. The question, then, is how to trace through the various mechanisms which render the suppression of heterosexual desire persuasive in Wordsworth's poetry.

One such organization is that enforcing in men an opposition between the Madonna and the Whore. Instituted in many cultures under different names as the opposition between Eros and Agape, Love Sacred and Profane, this is an ideological dichotomy with a psychic component. Both the little girl and the little boy start by being equally active in seeking the (symbolic) mother, but, whereas the little girl moves (if she does) from the mother as object, to the father, to another adult man, the little boy moves (if he does) directly from the mother to another adult woman. Because love of the mother and desire for the other woman trench so intimately upon each other, men have to work harder to keep the two feelings apart. All are liable in a measure to the form of neurosis Freud describes some men suffering because 'Where they love they do not desire and where they desire they do not love'. Wordsworth suffers very badly. In *The Prelude* he declares how, coming to London:

> I heard, and for the first time in my life,
> The voice of woman utter blasphemy –
> Saw woman as she is to open shame
> Abandoned, and the pride of public vice;
> I shuddered, for a barrier seemed at once
> Thrown in, that from humanity divorced
> Humanity, splitting the race of man
> In twain, yet leaving the same outward form.
>
> *(VII: 383–91)*

'Woman as she is'? 'Splitting the race of man'? This passage is entirely consistent with the rest of Wordsworth's writing in which heterosexual desire for the adult woman is surrendered in favour of an idealized, desexualized image deriving from the mother and projected onto the sister as well. As has been argued already here, not only does Wordsworth refuse to give up his place as object of the desire of the mother, he has also found poetic means to refer to guilt and paternal law while imaging them in terms of landscape and the maternal body.

The phallic father

If every human subject retains the capacity for both heterosexual and homosexual desire such that the choice of an object is never ever more than a preference, then it is reasonable to look for male figures in Wordsworth's poetry which, as well as being points for narcissistic identification, are objects of homosexual desire. One does not have to look far. A single male figure stalks through Wordsworth's poetry always with the same set of features. Isolated, tall and erect, he is either standing or walking often with a long staff in his hand – the old Cumberland beggar in that poem, the Leech-gatherer in 'Resolution and Independence' who appears like 'a huge stone' or 'a sea-beast', the discharged soldier (*The Prelude*) who was:

> A span above man's common measure, tall,
> Stiff, lank, and upright . . .   (*IV: 392–3*)

or the blind beggar seen in London who, with 'upright face, / Stood, propped against a wall' (VII: 639–40).

This idealized male object is particularly represented by the shepherd as in *The Prelude*:

> A rambling schoolboy, thus,
> I felt his presence in his own domain,
> As of a lord and master, or a power,
> Or genius, under Nature, under God,
> Presiding; and severest solitude
> Had more commanding looks when he was there.
> When up the lonely brooks on rainy days
> Angling I went, or trod the trackless hills
> By mists bewildered, suddenly mine eyes
> Have glanced upon him distant a few steps,
> In size a giant, stalking through thick fog,
> His sheep like Greenland bears; or, as he stepped
> Beyond the boundary line of some hill-shadow,
> His form hath flashed upon me, glorified
> By the deep radiance of the setting sun:
> Or him have I descried in distant sky,
> A solitary object and sublime,
> Above all height! like an aerial cross
> Stationed alone upon a spiry rock
> Of the Chartreuse, for worship. Thus was man
> Ennobled outwardly before my sight . . .
> (*VIII: 256–7*)

Size seems to be everything. With 'commanding looks' (a castrating gaze) and a body enhanced by the sun's rays, the shepherd starts as a giant and grows until he is as big as a mountain peak. Michael, in the poem of that name, is another shepherd and the good father, similarly imagined:

> And, truly, at all times, the storm, that drives
> The traveller to a shelter, summoned him
> Up to the mountains: he had been alone

Amid the heart of many thousand mists,
That came to him, and left him, on the heights . . .

Wordsworth's preferred man is not just big, he's also hard – seemingly impervious to wind, rain, sleet and mist, particularly mist. In both these little narratives the hero comes into sharp focus as a distinct and defined entity with firm edges by emerging out of an element whose property is to blur and efface boundaries. Since the shepherd is outstandingly masculine, it would not be fanciful to suppose this mist to be feminized in contrast. The Happy Warrior in the poem of that name is also 'lifted high' as a 'Conspicuous object in a Nation's eye', and wins 'Heaven's applause' just when 'the moral mist is gathering'.

Fantasy cannot be separated from history and ideology, for in pre-Modern society the role of the phallic father in the collective imagination of Western society was, naturally, taken by the Christian God, son of no-one and Father of all. With secularization at the Renaissance the position is taken by the king but that option is ruled out after the French Revolution (if not the English one of the seventeenth century). In this respect Wordsworth's casting of the common man in the role of phallic father is radically democratic though obviously only within a traditionally patriarchal framework. This figure is still very much alive today. In the film 'Dirty Harry' Clint Eastwood is a detective obsessed with destroying a bisexual murderer; at the end as the killer forces a school bus to turn off the motorway he looks up to see the stiff and upright figure of Eastwood standing on a road-bridge, outlined against the sunset. Wordsworth's shepherd, his form similarly glorified by the sun, is a Romantic original for this pervasive contemporary image.

Empson says that Wordsworth used 'the mountains as a totem or father-substitute' but things are not that simple because there is always more than one motive at work in fantasy. Although Wordsworth's special object can be confidently identified as the phallic father, varying kinds of position towards him are available, including fetishism, sublimation and identification.

Wordsworth's man-mountain has many of the attributes of a fetish. Fetishism, which typifies men rather than women, occurs when a fantasy object is erected in place of the phallus imagined to be missing from the mother's body. Lack can seem to be made up for if the father is staged as huge, substantial, firm, clearly defined in outline and without broken edges, solid rather than liquid, fixed rather than variable – above all seemingly autonomous and self-sufficient, an unmoved mover. Wordsworth's shepherds are fetishized to the extent that they are accorded these features though they mean other things as well.

The phallic father may be an object of male homosexual desire, though over this it is important to distinguish between repressed and sublimated desire. While desire which is repressed is always likely to return, sublimation can transform its force and affect. Desire withdrawn onto the ego becomes desexualized when it is directed to an aim other than that of sexual satisfaction. So it is with art, for example. Paintings of desirable objects transform that desire by presenting it in the socially acceptable form of fantasies the I can know and deliberately enjoy. The male bond largely consists of homosexual desire which has been sublimated through mutual identification and identification with a socially valuable purpose, 'Liberty, equality and fraternity' for instance. That is very like the feeling Wordsworth records in Book X of *The Prelude* when his friendship with Beaupuy is at its most intense and his sense of comradeship strongest – no man is a stranger to him.

While the phallic father in Wordsworth's earlier stages is taken as a fetish or object of desire, the feeling that comes to dominate is, suitably enough, identification. Even at Cambridge, Wordsworth reflects:

> Hitherto I had stood
> In my own mind remote from social life,
> (At least from what we commonly so name,)
> Like a lone shepherd on a promontory,
> Who lacking occupation looks far forth
> Into the boundless sea, and rather makes
> Than finds what he beholds.
>
> (*III: 513–19*)

Here water, the sea, performs the effect of mist elsewhere, and there is the extraordinary idea that this sovereign gaze actually produces what is seen, as, in the ancient fantasy, a god's breath or speech creates the world. In Book XIV *The Prelude* culminates in the story of Wordsworth climbing Mount Snowdon. From the top he sees the Atlantic:

> The Moon hung naked in a firmament
> Of azure without cloud, and at my feet
> Rested a silent sea of hoary mist.
> A hundred hills their dusky backs upheaved
> All over this still ocean; and beyond,
> Far, far beyond, the solid vapours stretched,
> In headlands, tongues, and promontory shapes,
> Into the main Atlantic, that appeared
> To dwindle, and give up his majesty,
> Usurped upon far as the sight could reach.
>
> (*XIV: 40–49*)

If earlier the figure of the shepherd emerges from the mist, here it is Wordsworth; if earlier, for example in the boat-stealing incident, it is as though he is chased by a man-mountain, 'a huge peak, black and huge' (I: 378), now it is as though he has become that mountain. He now possesses the phallic gaze which can penetrate the moonlight, seeing for miles and miles, out into the ocean, even, so it is hinted, materially altering ('Usurped') what it sees.

Identification, a form of narcissistic drive, redirects desire by turning it back through the ego, sublimating it (to use the technical term). That process is fundamental in Wordsworth's poetry for it promises a means to deal with sexual desire, both homosexual and heterosexual, by turning it into self-love. A paradigm of this effect is given in the one moment in *The Prelude* in which Wordsworth admits to feeling sexual desire. As an eighteen-year-old virgin he goes to a party in his summer vacation and experiences 'Slight shocks of young love-liking' (IV: 17), finds his heart full 'to the brim' but manages to avoid spilling anything by getting married to himself:

> I made no vows, but vows
> Were then made for me; bond unknown to me
> Was given, that I should be, else sinning greatly,
> A dedicated Spirit.
>
> *(IV: 334–7)*

Through this process in which he identifies with the flattering idea of being a 'dedicated Spirit', love for the other, construed as 'sinning greatly', is transformed into love for himself.

Narcissism and desire

Wordsworth wishes to be the phallus. In the 'Tintern Abbey' poem he identifies with a power that 'impels' all objects, in 'Elegiac Stanzas' with a 'huge Castle, standing here' which is 'cased in . . . unfeeling armour' and 'braves' external threat. In *The Prelude* childhood sits 'on a throne' which has 'more power' than the elements (V: 508–509); regaining his true self Wordsworth says he 'stood' in Nature's presence 'as now I stand' (XII: 206); he recognizes that 'simple childhood' is the base on which 'stands' the greatness of man (XII: 274–5). Dedicated to the 'power' of imagination, he wants to be imagination, as in the evocation of imagination after crossing the Alps:

> Imagination – here the Power so called
> Through sad incompetence of human speech,
> That awful Power rose from the mind's abyss

Like an unfathered vapour that enwraps,
At once, some lonely traveller . . .

(VI: 592–6)

More than one critic has been struck by the word 'unfathered' here.
Marlon Ross points out that Wordsworth 'does not use the word
"unmothered"' even though it is linguistically feasible 'because he is
not so much referring here to the birth or origin as to the final cause
that ordains and justifies existence itself'. Mary Jacobus says that
Wordsworth's likening of himself to an unfathered vapour is 'a rejection
of the Oedipus complex – hence a claim to found the self'. All this
'power', 'strength' and capacity to 'stand' which Wordsworth seeks to
adopt repeats a single idea – that he might be the phallus, cause of all
and effect of nothing.

It is only an apparent paradox that to be the phallus entails desexualiza-
tion, that a gain in seeming omnipotence is purchased at the price of
a loss of sexual identity, both homosexual and heterosexual desire. Once
again an example from popular culture and mass fantasy helps clarify
the question (and shows these themes are active now, not just then).
In the movies, Superman, who unquestionably signifies the phallus
(omnipotent, able to fly, etc.), cannot desire Lois Lane though his mature
alter ego, Clark Kent, can. That theme is explicit in 'Superman II', when
Superman, in order to love Lois, must surrender his transcendent powers.
To be the phallus is to be desexualized, losing differentiated sexual
identity like the polymorphously perverse infant. It in this context
I would read the critical commonplace that Wordsworth exhibits both
traditionally feminine and masculine aspects, both gentleness and soft-
ness as well as strength and power. However, he does not just want to
be the phallus – he wants to have the phallus as well. He wants, that is,
to see and know himself as the phallus, to see himself seeing himself.
These attributes of seeing and knowing reintroduce the usual modes
of inherited masculinity.

A more conventional way to pose this question would be via a contrast
between Milton and Wordsworth, between Miltonic aggression and
Wordsworthian pliancy, a contrast going right down to the harsh clang
of Miltonic consonants versus Wordsworth's mild deployment of labials
and palatals ('Till all was tranquil as a dreamless sleep', The Prelude, I: 463,
for instance). Another way would be to contrast Wordsworth's phallic
fathers with those so widely and fiercely promoted in contemporary
culture – Dirty Harry, Superman, Rambo – on the grounds that
Wordsworth's show a marked absence of aggression. Since aggression
is particularly a function of the I (structured, ultimately, by the insistence
that it is everything and the other is nothing) and since Wordsworth's

poetry is profoundly narcissistic in theme and effect, what one may ask has happened to the concomitant aggression? The answer – an answer – is, I think, that the aggression is mainly directed back against the self, a version of the self. Wordsworth, so it was argued in the previous two chapters, mourns his former self; a lost self which is kept alive through the identification with it of the subject's I on condition that another, more conscious self is critical and accordingly aggressive in seeing, watching, guarding that former self. There is aggression in Wordsworth but it has been displaced into this form of mourning for the lost object. Sexual desire and the idea of woman imagined (in the traditional scenario) as cause of that desire get caught up in this aggressive mourning.

However forcibly the subject tries to be at one with itself by living out the structures of narcissism, sublimation and self-love, the other remains. For the would-be self-sufficient masculine self there is still the problem of sexual difference and the feminine other. In the end, with his back to the wall, Wordsworth deals with it – would deal with it – in a particularly drastic way, one which dredges up strategies from some of the most archaic levels of patriarchy and makes them acceptable in polite conversation.

Writing of Hollywood cinema in an article which has since provoked an entire bookshelf of feminist scholarship, Laura Mulvey takes up Freud's suggestion that patriarchal culture is characterized by *horror feminae* and men's 'dread of women'. Such dread is founded in the fantasy that everyone is phallic so that women have projected onto them the fears their apparent lack provokes in men. Mulvey proposes that 'the male unconscious has two avenues of escape' from this imagined threat, either 're-enactment of the original trauma (investigating the woman, demystifying her mystery), counterbalanced by the devaluation, punishment or saving of the guilty object' or 'turning the represented figure itself into a fetish so that it becomes reassuring rather than dangerous'. A crude paraphrase would say that patriarchy must narrativize woman into an object either dead or married (an option reinforced in countless Hollywood films). Since Wordsworth clearly does not fetishize women, the only alternative, on this showing, is to master them through investigation and punishment. This is how we may read the following example.

'She was a Phantom of Delight'

She was a Phantom of delight
When first she gleamed upon my sight;
A lovely Apparition, sent
To be a moment's ornament;

Her eyes as stars of Twilight fair;
Like Twilight's, too, her dusky hair;
But all things else about her drawn
From May-time and the cheerful Dawn;
A dancing Shape, an Image gay,
To haunt, to startle, and way-lay.

I saw her upon nearer view,
A Spirit, yet a Woman too!
Her household motions light and free,
And steps of virgin-liberty;
A countenance in which did meet
Sweet records, promises as sweet;
A Creature not too bright or good
For human nature's daily food;
For transient sorrows, simple wiles,
Praise, blame, love, kisses, tears, and smiles.

And now I see with eye serene
The very pulse of the machine;
A Traveller between life and death;
The reason firm, the temperate will,
Endurance, foresight, strength and skill;
A perfect Woman, nobly planned,
To warn, to comfort, and command;
And yet a Spirit still, and bright
With something of angelic light.

There isn't much in the way of desire here, or rather, there is but
it is expressed as the desire for mastery. At first she is the other, a
'Phantom', an 'Apparition', a 'Shape', 'an Image', a 'Spirit' – in process,
labile, undefined, or at least not definable by him. But he works at
it – she's a virgin and good at housework – and so he begins to become
able to see and know her as his eye penetrates her. In the third verse
he sees 'with eye serene / The very pulse of the machine' (if his gaze is
now 'serene' if must have been troubled before); she is a 'Traveller
between life and death' (but the Leech-gatherer wasn't that, for he
seems to 'pace / About the weary moors continually'); this woman is
safe (made safe) when she is transformed into an object of knowledge
(not desire), an object which, as an object of knowledge, is effectively
inert, dead.

It seems impossible for Wordsworth to think of a woman without
thinking of her as dead. 'To a Young Lady, who had been reproached for
taking long walks in the country' starts out innocently enough but ends
up by imagining how a serene old age will 'lead thee to thy grave'; the
story of 'Laodamia' ends up with Laodamia lying 'on the palace-floor

a lifeless corse'; Lucy Gray, in that poem, sets out to walk home in the snow and dies in an icy stream. Even a sonnet to a river, the River Duddon, begins:

> I thought of Thee, my partner and my guide
> As being past away . . .

And another, which William Wordsworth probably wrote about the death of his daughter at three, takes up the tone and manner of Milton writing about his dead wife:

> Surprised by joy – impatient as the Wind
> I turned to share the transport – Oh! with whom
> But Thee, deep buried in the silent tomb . . .

In the sonnet which starts 'Methought I saw my late espoused Saint' Milton has a vision of a dead woman brought back from the grave: Wordsworth turns to speak to his companion, imagining she's alive, only to recall that she is dead.

Going back to Petrarch (who wrote 263 poems to Laura 'In Vita' and another 102 to her when she was dead) and beyond to the poetry of Courtly Love, there stretches a line of masculinized love poetry in which the woman is addressed as an object, perfect, fixed, eternal (and thus held firmly in her allocated place). Being in love appears to close the gap between the self and the Other: 'love is essentially deception', introducing 'a perspective centred on the Ideal point, capital I, placed somewhere in the Other, from which the Other sees me, in the form I like to be seen'. That is: in speaking about the supposedly perfect woman a man installs her figure in the place of an ideal, using it to see himself reflected at his best and as he hopes others see him – the perfect lover. The five Wordsworth texts grouped as the 'Lucy' poems develop this organization to an extreme but in a way consistent with the rest of his presentation of sexuality and gender.

In 'Strange fits of passion have I known' the I of the poem recounts how he rode on his horse to his lover's cottage one evening. He began to watch the moon in a state of trance-like obsession as it sank; suddenly it disappeared from sight behind her house and the thought (wish) comes to him, 'If Lucy should be dead'. 'She dwelt among the untrodden ways' recalls Lucy as a Maid (virgin) who lived where there were 'none to praise' her and 'very few to love' her, yet for him she is like a 'violet by a mossy stone' or a star when it is the only one in the sky; in life she was unknown and few could know when she died, but, as he says:

> . . . she is in her grave, and, oh,
> The difference to me!

The question does not arise of how Lucy may have felt about living where there were few to love and none to praise her – he is only too happy with the reassurance he has her all to himself. In 'Three years she grew' Nature speaks of Lucy's virtues, especially her capacity to be at one with the external world:

> And hers shall be the breathing balm,
> And hers the silence and the calm
> Of mute insensate things.

Hardly has Nature spoken when Lucy dies, leaving to him:

> The memory of what has been,
> And never more will be.

Lucy is also dead at the end of 'I travelled among unknown men'. He thinks of England from abroad and of Lucy left at home with her spinning wheel but in an equation between Nature, England and Lucy, one which implies but doesn't state her death, England contains 'the last green field / That Lucy's eyes surveyed'.

In each of these Lucy is – or is thought of – as dead; each is structured around regret, on the model discussed in the chapters on autobiography, for her actual absence makes it possible to keep her present through memory. When Lucy died she 'left . . . the memory of what has been' and though this trace also recalls the absence of its original (she 'never more will be') it is as though a real object has been bequeathed – left – to the speaker, the remembering subject. In order to keep things clear it's worth the risk of schematizing the effect:

1 In death Lucy becomes at one with Nature, the subject/object dyad becomes hermetically sealed and though Lucy is not fortunate enough to experience this for herself, the speaker, can, in retrospect. A politics of gender would point to the way the threat (to him) of her otherness is reduced to the extent that she has become a 'mute insensate' thing.

2 Dead, perfected in memory, like Petrarch's Laura, she can be idealized and he – who loved her as she loved him – idealized along with her (rather as in some altar-pieces the portrait of the kneeling donor can be seen in the corner of the picture).

3 As a remembered object, a kind of photograph, he as a subject can hope to see himself reflected in her – all the more easily because she represents the dyadic unity of the two of them.

4 The process of mourning introduces a split in his subjectivity: while his I, in identification with her (them), becomes passive, his self-consciousness can see, know and recognize her (them). Part of him

is identified with her, and so, in the same structure as that with which autobiography treats a remembered self, her dead body becomes like his own dead self and he can hope therefore to see himself. According to this necrophilic logic, if she is the phallus and he identifies with her, he can both be the phallus and have the phallus if he can possess her through knowledge.

5 In presenting himself to the reader as the noble and grief-smitten lover, he can hope to be seen as he would like, to this extent once again trying to fulfil the wish to see himself seeing himself.

A fifth poem, the best known, is short enough to recall in full:

> A slumber did my spirit seal;
>   I had no human fears:
> She seemed a thing that could not feel
>   The touch of earthly years.
>
> No motion has she now, no force;
>   She neither hears nor sees;
> Rolled round in earth's diurnal course,
>   With rocks, and stones, and trees.

Is the sealing of his spirit like the seal on a document adding to its security or a seal which shuts off and closes? If he had no 'human' fears, perhaps he should have since we are all mortal? To be 'a thing that could not feel' might be to be dead though to seem such, especially if immune to ageing, rather connotes the opposite – immortality. Yet whatever uncertainties are triggered by the first stanza, they are decisively resolved in the second: the poem dramatizes knowledge passing from one state to another, from a past to a present ('now'). Lucy's transcendence in the first stanza is recognized to have been seen only through the eyes of love, an appearance now recognized to have been an appearance from a position which, accordingly, can claim to know the truth.

Paul de Man, in a shrewd and suggestive way, has considered how this best-known of the 'Lucy' poems works, as well as indicating some of its gender implications:

> . . . the poem is written from the point of view of a unified self that fully recognises a past condition as one of error and stands in a present that, however painful, sees things as they actually are. This stance has been made possible by two things: first, the death alluded to is not the death of the speaker but apparently that of someone else; second, the poem is in the third person and uses the feminine gender throughout.

What this criticism rightly picks up is the (would-be) absolute mastery that the speaker exacts. That certainty, that adopted position of exteriority able to look on and know, is produced also by the operation of the text, especially the precise, carefully sustained syntax, and it is to the question of Wordsworth's language that the next chapter will turn.

Wordsworth's self-ascribed power, his narcissistic mastery, his hard and unflinching gaze, his demand to know for certain, his steely determination to have the phallus – all have as their necessary condition a corresponding silence and inertia of the object frozen for inspection, mute and insensate. And the absolutely silent and inert woman is a dead one, as Sarah Kofman explains:

> To make a dead body of woman is to try one last time to overcome her enigmatic and ungraspable character, to fix in a definite and immovable position instability and mobility themselves ... for women's death-like rigidity ... makes it possible to put an end to the perpetual shifting back and forth between masculinity and femininity which constitutes the whole enigma of 'woman'.

A similar comment is made in a harsher fashion by Leslie Fiedler when, summing up the attitude towards sexuality in *Uncle Tom's Cabin*, he writes that 'The only safe woman is a dead woman'. So it is also in Wordsworth's poetry.

7

Language

With this goes a theory that 'natural', i.e.
conversational language is better, and therefore
more poetic than 'artificial', i.e. literary
language. He (Wordsworth) does not see that
both are equally artificial, i.e. directed to a
social end – and equally natural, i.e. products of
man's struggle with Nature.

Christopher Caudwell

Although it does not have the same kind of materiality as some other things (why should it?), language is material. It is physical in that no communication between two people can take place without a physical contact of some kind (sound waves, telephone-wire, tape for tape-recorder, paper and pencil, screen of a word-processor) and it is material in that meaning (the signified) cannot be produced except by means of a shaped sound (the signifier). The so-called 'words on the page' actually consist of graphic reproduction of a set of signifiers which could as well be reproduced by someone speaking them on a video-recording or on CD or reading them aloud to a room full of people. By following the rules of a given language, readers in the present produce signifieds from the signifiers they come across. Whatever particular set of signifiers was put in order then, we produce meanings from them now. Epitomizing this, Michael Westlake's novel, *51 Soko*, portrays Prince Genji, the hero of the ancient Japanese romance, as a subject who only comes properly alive when someone is reading about him. Like Prince Genji, Wordsworth relies completely on us and future generations to lend his writing existence and meaning, although of course its written feature ensures it will always go beyond anything we read from it as it is brought alive (one hopes) by future readers.

Wordsworth believes that language is by nature transparent to thought (intentions, meanings, experiences) and if it isn't, it ought to be. In a passage from 'Essays upon Epitaphs' which I am not the first to quote he affirms:

> Words are too awful an instrument for good and evil to be trifled with: they hold above all other external powers a dominion over thoughts. if words be not (recurring to a metaphor before used) an incarnation of the thought but only a clothing for it, then surely will they prove an ill gift; such a one as those poisoned vestments, read of in the stories of superstitious times, which had power to consume and to alienate from his right mind the victim who put them on. Language, if it do not uphold, and feed, and leave in quiet, like the power of gravitation or the air we breathe, is a counter-spirit, unremittingly and noiselessly at work to derange, to subvert, to lay waste, to vitiate, and to dissolve.

Words should not be physical and material, an addition to meaning (clothing), but, as Jesus was to God, an 'incarnation' of thought, as clear to meaning as 'the air we breathe' so that meaning just passes through it. On the evidence of this passage Wordsworth becomes hysterical at any prospect of the alternative. The fact that the materiality of the signifier always resists impregnation by thought, quite simply that words will always mean something different to someone else however hard you try to fill them with your own ideas, fills him with horror, not only because it threatens to divide the self from its supposed fullness and 'right mind', but, by the same token, because it seems an attack on his manhood, as when Hercules, prompted by his wife Deianira, put on a shirt saturated with some kind of acid. This impossible dream of a wordless language is fleshed out in the 'Preface'.

The 'Preface' to *Lyrical Ballads*

A poet, so this prose defence of the early poems proposes, has greater power than others 'in expressing what he thinks and feels'. The concept of expression assumes that the inward can be made outward without any change, like toothpaste expressed from a tube; thought can be made outward in words because it passes through language like light through a glass window: 'poetry is the spontaneous overflow of powerful feelings'. Since language hardly interferes with this expression or overflow, the 'Preface' makes no distinction between language in general and the particular form of it which is poetry – there 'neither is, nor can be, any *essential* difference between the language of prose and metrical composition'. With this move all the specific effects of poetry that depend on a particular deployment of the signifier – being written in lines would be a main instance – simply fall away. These are accidental while the essence of poetry consists of feelings or experiences translated directly across from life into art as the meaning of poetry.

To support this position the 'Preface' discriminates between good and bad poetry. Poetry which reminds us of the signifier is bad. At a stroke the rhetorical tradition stretching back to ancient Greece is abolished and the way cleared to define good poetry as unmarked not just by rhetoric but by the signifier at all – 'all good poetry *is* the spontaneous overflow of powerful feelings' (italics added). Since the position remains indefensible, various manoeuvres are carried out to protect it. The 'Preface' tries not to admit that life and art, experience and the poetic representation of experience, are different. Poetry must 'fall short of that which is uttered by men in real life', though this concedes only a difference in degree, not in kind. Wordsworth goes on to admit what he must: 'However exalted a notion we would wish to cherish of the character of a Poet, it is obvious, that, while he describes and imitates passions, his situation is in some degree slavish and mechanical, compared with the freedom and power of real and substantial action and suffering'.

That concession is made only to be immediately recuperated. Though in comparison with life poetry is 'mechanical', the poet must try to overcome this if he or she can. Inevitably, the signifier remains unaccounted for, notably the fact that poetry is written in lines comparable purely in terms of patterns of sound, not of meaning. So, compelled by the logic of his own argument, Wordsworth asks, 'Why, professing these opinions, have I written in verse?' The question is devastating and the answer gives it all away: writing in lines, according to parallelism in the organization of the signifier, has nothing essential to do with poetry but yields a pleasurable supplement, happening to 'superadd' a 'charm'. This qualification unravels the whole argument for the 'Preface' means us to overlook the signifier altogether.

No matter how he wriggles, there is no way Wordsworth can get the 'poison' of the signifier out of the system of language. What he can do, of course, is offer us a poetry which seeks to efface its own materiality. I find it an extraordinary irony, then, that a writer who so passionately hoped to make the word immaterial in the face of feeling should be named WORDS WORTH. Here I shall hope to show that the self, imagination and pathos – key feelings and experiences in Wordsworth's poetry – all come to us only on the basis of a rhetoric of the self, a rhetoric of imagination and a rhetoric of pathos.

The rhetoric of the self

The two passages that follow, both describing scenery, are for the sake of comparison – the first from a pretty conventional late eighteenth-century poem of natural description:

> The loitering traveller hence, at evening, sees
> From rock-hewn steps the sail between the trees;
> Or marks, 'mid opening cliffs, fair dark-eyed maids
> Tend the small harvest of their garden glades;
> Or stops the solemn mountain-shades to view
> Stretch o'er the pictured mirror broad and blue,
> And track the yellow lights from steep to steep,
> As up the opposing hills they slowly creep.
> Aloft, here, half a village shines, arrayed
> In golden light; half hides itself in shade:
> While from amid the darkened roofs, the spire,
> Restlessly flashing, seems to mount like fire:
> There, all unshaded, blazing forests throw
> Rich golden verdure on the lake below.
> Slow glides the sail along the illumined shore,
> And steals into the shade the lazy oar;
> Soft bosoms breathe around contagious sighs,
> And amorous music on the water dies.

Corresponding to the mastering rationalism of the Enlightenment is an equally universalizing and controlled sentimentalism. The view is self-consciously screened segment by segment for objects of visual pleasure. Fixed as a given, like a painting, the landscape and figures are displayed for the dominating gaze of the I who masters it. Unnamed and unmarked, the speaker is subsumed into 'the loitering traveller', a typical figure, who in turn is subsumed into a general eye (or I). What is 'here' and what is 'There' discriminate attributes of the object rather than admit the situation of the viewing subject. One 'half' of a village hides while a balancing 'half' shines, as in Pope's *Windsor Forest* (see pp. 9–10): the variegated order is supposedly out there. Since the object is always already known all the poem can do is render it as accurately as possible for a typical subject. The ideal is transparency, letting the real shine through the words.

Of course this cannot be done and a strategy for recuperation is deployed. The couplet form, though often thought to let the signifier obtrude, works, I would argue, in the opposite direction. Because of its obviously repetitive form the couplet pulls the chain of meaning endlessly forward across and through the rhyming pairs, at the same time, through its firm grid of expectation, ensuring no departure from a gentlemanly, moderated tone – the voice of he who is supposed to know.

Since you can't elude the signifier anyway, the couplet form would, as it were, make the best of a bad job, by dealing with it all at once at the end of the line. And, in this usage, the rhyme word tries to make sound echo sense, hold the signifier onto a meaning assumed to be there first.

In this respect it really doesn't matter that the word-order is not that of speech ('And steals into the shade the lazy oar' instead of 'the lazy oar steals into the shade') or that the vocabulary is obviously conventional and shared (the use of the definite article – 'the yellow lights', 'the lazy oar' – confirming that the generalized, typifying adjective is suitable for the noun). The passage shows entire confidence that the signifier can be subordinated to signified, made appropriate to it, and so prevented from interfering with transparent representation.

Whereas the extract from this descriptive poem aims to contain the signifier so as to state for a universal subject what is, the following Wordsworth poem, published in 1815, suggests that its project is to get rid of the signifier altogether in the name of 'individual experience':

> 'A Night-Piece'
> The sky is overcast
> With a continuous cloud of texture close,
> Heavy and wan, all whitened by the Moon,
> Which through that veil is indistinctly seen,
> A dull, contracted circle, yielding light
> So feebly spread, that not a shadow falls,
> Chequering the ground – from rock, plant, tree, or tower.
> At length a pleasant instantaneous gleam
> Startles the pensive traveller while he treads
> His lonesome path, with unobserving eye
> Bent earthwards; he looks up – the clouds are split
> Asunder, – and above his head he sees
> The clear Moon, and the glory of the heavens.
> There, in a black-blue vault she sails along,
> Followed by multitudes of stars, that, small
> And sharp, and bright, along the dark abyss
> Drive as she drives: how fast they wheel away,
> Yet vanish not! – the wind is in the tree,
> But they are silent; – still they roll along
> Immeasurably distant; and the vault,
> Built round by those white clouds, enormous clouds,
> Still deepens its unfathomable depth.
> At length the Vision closes; and the mind,
> Not undisturbed by the delight it feels,
> Which slowly settles into peaceful calm,
> Is left to muse upon the solemn scene.

Blank verse in the poem constitutes a necessary condition for something very different. The paragraph begins – and ends – in terms fairly close to those of the previous extract. The traveller is not loitering but pensive, and the effect of seeing the moon is left muted and unexplored (he is 'Not undisturbed'). But across this breaks the rendering of an individual located in a particular time and place, a domain of personal subjectivity rather than universal knowledge, his mastery temporarily undone by an unconscious irruption. Instead of being inverted to support the demand for a rhyme, the word-order follows the sequence of everyday speech; instead of trying to work up an elaborated and conventional sense of appropriate nouns and adjectives ('garden glades', 'blazing forests') the phrasing accepts an almost banal, everyday phrasing (the moon is 'clear', the stars are 'bright', the sky is 'silent', the clouds 'white') but one profoundly altered by its contextualization.

This is not in heroic couplets but blank verse. Unrhymed iambic metre allows syntactic progression to be either disrupted or extended so as to express direct, present experience (the effect of that). Instead of 'he looks up and sees' we get a sentence interjected, 'the clouds are split / Asunder', a sudden, rhythmically urgent monosyllabic phrasing which represents the clouds as though being seen now. The moon is described not as it is but as it is perceived, watched as it 'sails along', then seen to be 'Followed by multitudes of stars', then these are noticed as 'small' and 'sharp' and 'bright', each adjective separated and added like an afterthought giving an effect as though the syntactical chain were being prolonged in the present in response to what is being looked at now. Further variations in intonation, pace and syntactic manipulation follow – the stars, the moon felt as wheeling in relation to the passing cloud, the wind, the silence, the perceived movement again, then the eye moving back to the clouds which are redefined in the act of being observed: at first said to be 'white clouds', they are immediately redescribed as 'enormous clouds', the repetition aiming to express the intensity of a mind experiencing in the present. Whereas in the earlier passage the demonstratives 'here' and 'There' referred out to features of the object, in 'A Night-Piece' demonstratives insist on the presence of an I supposedly here for the moon which is 'There' relative to this I, for which the stars 'still' roll along as they did a couple of lines – and seconds – earlier.

It would be very easy indeed to rewrite this paragraph from third-person concern with a 'pensive traveller' into the first-person. Just as the unnamed speaker who recounts the traveller's experience becomes invisibly identified with him, so the reader of 'A Night-Piece' is invited to find himself or herself mirrored in the he who narrates. Because of the rhetorical effects the operation of the signifier in the ways described here – avoidance of obviously conventional phrasing, expressively variable syntax, rendering of perceptions changing through time in a specifically located place – the passage is able to represent an I perceiving, narrating, experiencing. There is no such I unless the reader provides him by responding actively to the marks of the text.

In the cinema we are familiar with a point-of-view shot. Woken in the night by a loud noise the young woman in a horror film, instead of locking her door tight and staying in bed, picks up her candle and sets off to investigate. A camera arranged at head-height films while tracking through sets of gloomy corridors and craning down dark stairs; shown after an image of the heroine as she leaves her room, this gives the effect of seeing what she sees as she sees it. In the cinema there is no woman in nightclothes, no candle, no castle, no progress towards a darkened and draughty room (in which the candle blows out) – only light shining through treated celluloid so the projection enlarges the image on a screen. Similarly, in Wordsworth's poem there is no moon, no sky, no clouds, no traveller, no mind experiencing the nightscape, no I – there are only traces, an organization of signifiers from which the reader in the present produces the effect of a self experiencing the natural world. The presence of a speaker for 'A Night-Piece', like that in most of Wordsworth's poems, depends upon a text, which, like the script of a play – better, a soliloquy in Hamlet – is well constructed and lends itself to a convincing performance.

The first passage – the unremarkable eighteenth-century landscape – was in fact by William Wordsworth, from his *Descriptive Sketches* of 1793. 'A Night-Piece', written in 1798, evidences an advance not in the capacity to feel more spontaneously but rather in techniques of representation. While *Descriptive Sketches* wants to maintain a rhetoric in which the signifier seems to fit the signified, 'A Night-Piece' hopes to be done with the signifier altogether, that the rendering of an experiencing consciousness can provide such a vivid script the reader will not notice how far it falls short of 'real and substantial action and suffering'. The reader feels entitled to go directly to the experience of the represented I (whose delight settles into calm) because the text is arranged so as to encourage this. The presence of the self depends on a poem which pretends not to be a poem, a text effacing its own textuality. That is the persistent effect in Wordsworth's poetry after 1798 and in the whole tradition of expressive representation since then.

The rhetoric of the imagination

The effect of the self, of an individual thinking and experiencing, derives from an organization of the signifier but it is also produced by the use of a certain kind of metaphor. This, more than anything else, gave currency to the term 'imagination' at the time of the Romantic movement, a currency which has become almost universally accepted down to the present-day. There has always been a huge amount of loose talk about the imagination. A generation ago when I was a student I tried very hard to get hold of a precise and comprehensible definition of imagination but without success (at least so I remember it). Now, I think the word can be explained, particularly as it pertains to Wordsworth's poetry.

While traditionally imagination had been a fairly neutral term to mean having something present in your mind – the sense in which Hamlet refers to the idea of Yorick's skull being 'abhorred in my imagination' – with Romanticism it collected a whole new load of meanings. In the 'Preface,' to *Lyrical Ballads* Wordsworth writes that incidents and situations have been treated in the poems by throwing over them 'a certain colouring of imagination' as though it were varnish over a painting. He clarifies this by saying that in the poems the feeling gives importance 'to the action and situation, and not the action and situation to the feeling', implying that what matters about the event or situation is how it is experienced subjectively. Coleridge in *Biographia Literaria* proclaims that primary imagination is perception, 'a repetition in the finite mind of the eternal act of creation in the infinite I AM', and that secondary or poetic imagination is an echo of this, a paragraph so portentously vague it well merits Catherine Belsey's sardonic summary: 'Subjectivity expands to fill the universe which it itself creates and which is then the object of its own knowledge'.

Coleridge goes on to say that imagination lends a sense of subjective vitality to objects which would otherwise be 'fixed and dead', a notion which becomes clearer when he writes specifically about poetic details. In a letter to Sotheby (10 September 1802) he states that 'a Poet's *Heart* & *Intellect* should be *combined*, *intimately* combined & *unified*, with the great appearances in Nature' and not merely mixed with those appearances through 'formal Similies' [sic]. Again, in *Biographia Literaria*, he says that for *Lyrical Ballads* his job (as distinct from Wordsworth's) was to write about supernatural characters in a way that was able 'to transfer from our inward nature a human interest' that would make them persuasive and plausible, in other words, to psychologize them. So far what we have is Coleridge's advocating the need for a sense of unity between subject and object, his own version of what Chapter 3 discusses as 'the Wordsworth experience'. However, as Coleridge further develops his account, with detailed examples, a new topic and possibility begins to appear.

Coleridge proposes that:

... images, however beautiful, though faithfully copied from nature, and as accurately represented in words, do not of themselves characterise the poet. They become proofs of original genius only ... when a human and intellectual life is transferred to them from the poet's own spirit.

He cites two lines,

Behold you row of pines, that shorn and bow'd
Bend from the sea-blast, seen at twilight eve,

and claims they begin to show these proofs of genius if they are modified with the idea that the pines are said to have 'all their tresses wild / Streaming before them'. Is the difference that the objects described now have subjective human qualities – streaming hair – attributed to them? It does not seem that simple, for Coleridge goes on to quote the Shakespeare sonnet (number 33) which begins:

Full many a glorious morning have I seen
Flatter the mountain tops with sovereign eye ...

The landscape has already been anthropomorphized by the attribution to the sun of an eye, but this is not what Coleridge especially picks up. Rather, it is the word 'Flatter', which, he says, is able to 'burst upon us at once in life and power'.

In attributing human attributes to the sun, why might this transference of subjective onto objective count as a proof of original genius? Suppose Coleridge's example read:

Full many a glorious morning have I seen
Approach the mountain tops with sovereign eye ...

There are good rhetorical reasons why the word 'flatter' is preferable to 'approach'. It yields more phonetic cohesion with the various /f/, /l/ and /t/ sounds in the surrounding context than would 'approach', and, in addition to the metaphorical equivalences THE SUN IS A FACE and THE SUN IS A KING (also weakly present in 'approach'), it brings in the hyperbole of the king flattering someone who thus borrows his glory. But it is not, I think, these rhetorical effects which lead Coleridge to say the word can 'burst upon us'. For over and above these, 'flatter' describes the landscape in an apparently unconventional, unpremeditated and unanticipated fashion. Granted that you are rendering in words the scene of early morning sunlight shining on hills, the word 'flatter' is able to make your response seem new and spontaneous while the word 'approach' can't.

Reading meanings into landscape – pathetic fallacy – is traditional enough, and Pope, for example, does just that in the passage earlier analysed from *Windsor Forest*. Romanticism psychologized schema shift to engage a sense of the subject/object dyad, as was the topic of Chapter 3. But now Coleridge is suggesting that what matters in the transfer of human life into images of nature lies rather in an exceptional or unusual use of metaphorical language, which by that token may claim to be at least a partial proof of original genius. All comparisons (whether metaphor or simile), insofar as they proceed from acts of comparing, necessarily implicate mind and subjectivity. Hence, *all* talk about landscapes using comparisons might be said to transfer subjective life to the objective world (which, as an earlier reference to Robbe-Grillet argued, may in any case be impossible to elude completely). At stake in imagination is not just the reading of meanings into landscape nor a Romantic sense of reciprocity between subject and object but in addition a kind of metaphorical expression able to give the effect that I am experiencing what is described as an individual rather than seeing what everyone sees. Individual subjectivity is to be reflected back in an object whose external difference and particularity, its hoped-for distance from any conventional sociality, will guarantee the uniqueness and originality of the I.

If I come up with a line to describe autumn in England:

October chestnuts falling on the pavement

it's so-so. Change it to:

October chestnuts exploding on the pavement

and it can at least lay some claim to be an original metaphor and so the expression of an individual who finds a similarity between chestnuts falling and bombs dropping. Wordsworth describes an animal on a spring day:

The hare is running races in her mirth;
And with her feet she from the plashy earth
Raises a mist; that, glittering in the sun,
Runs with her all the way, wherever she doth run.

An implied comparison is at work: the hare running is like another animal (a horse?) taking part in a race with others; drops of water thrown in the air from the sodden turf are like a mist; the mist and the imaginary competing animal are equated, the mist running with the hare 'wherever she doth run' (if the other animal is not a horse it's possibly the greyhound used for hare coursing, which indeed follows every twist and turn of its escaping prey). To the extent the developed comparison is original, it suggests individual experience.

When around 1800 Wordsworth and the others started to write poetry aiming to represent the spontaneous overflow of powerful individual feeling it was against the background of a tradition replete with conventional metaphors and similes, particularly from the old poetic game of anthropmorphizing the natural world. In the extract from *Windsor Forest* (see p. 10) woods which mingle light and shade are like a woman who says 'yes' and 'no' to her lover at once and fields with trees in them are said to be 'crown'd' by them; in *Descriptive Sketches* the lake is a 'mirror' for the sky and the church spire caught in the sun seems 'to mount like fire'. But as Charles Taylor notes, 'When Wordsworth and Hölderlin describe the natural world around us, in *The Prelude*, *The Rhine* or *Homecoming*, they no longer play on an established gamut of references, as Pope still could in Windsor Forest'. Wordsworth doesn't want to do that – he wants to celebrate the individual self seeing the world for itself and has worked up the rhetoric of the imagination as a way to give this effect. It is not just a question of establishing a sense of unity between subjective and objective domains but of trying to establish that unity on the basis of individual expression, to elude sociality altogether by what Raymond Williams terms 'a projection of personal feeling into a subjectively particularised and objectively generalised Nature'. The struggle is to work out ever-new comparisons for rendering a sense of external reality.

The broad theoretical difficulty with this is that if a use of language were authentically unique to an individual no-one else would ever know about it (there is no private language); in consequence, the Romantics face the local difficulty that expressive language of this kind becomes itself a convention, thus contradicting its own intention. When Wordsworth wrote

> I wandered lonely as a cloud
> That floats on high o'er vales and hills . . .

the description of himself and his state of mind was more or less originally rendered by the metaphor, A MAN WALKING ALONE IS A CLOUD. Two centuries later the situation is different. 'Strange Fruit' by Seamus Heaney opens with five metaphors:

> Here is the girl's head like an exhumed gourd.
> Oval-faced, prune-skinned, prune-stones for teeth.
> They unswaddled the wet fern of her hair
> And made an exhibition of its coil . . .

So we have: (1) a head (cut off as part of an ancient ritual and preserved in a museum) is like a gourd; (2) a head with black, wrinkled skin is like a prune or dried plum; (3) dead teeth are like small, black prune-stones;

(4) long hair unwrapped from the head is like swaddling clothes unwrapped from an infant; (5) hair which is long and thin and split into points is like wet fern. The four lines are stuffed with efforts to come up with original comparisons for aspects of the perceived world and so give a sense of the individual experiencing the described object for the first time. But can this be done or done any longer? Certainly now and arguably since around 1880 this whole Romantic tradition has itself become a worn-out convention – expressive language has become impossible (though no-one has told Seamus Heaney). What set out to be a personal act of imagination by escaping rhetoric ended up as a rhetoric of the imagination. But then it always was.

The rhetoric of pathos

A third form of rhetoric significantly at work in Wordsworth's poetry can be named as 'the rhetoric of pathos'. That rhetoric is much older and more widespread than simply its appearance in Wordsworth's poetry though its convincing deployment there explains much of the power and effect of some of his writing.

As has been insisted upon throughout, the subject is positioned by a text not just by what is said but mainly by how it is said, not so much on the plane of statement but on the plane of utterance – and uttering. This can be clearly exemplified in a poem which runs deliberately on the verge of parody. An unfinished work by Shelley begins:

> Death is here and death is there,
> Death is busy everywhere . . .

Not surprisingly entitled 'Death', the poem states meaning which is melancholy and unhappy but the jaunty rhythms and pat rhyme ensure that the words are spoken with an almost extravagant energy and life. Loss at one level, in the represented, is to be compensated for at another, in the performance, speaking or representation.

In the second chapter on autobiography it was argued that, following the psychoanalytic account of mourning and melancholy (see pp. 79–81), we should understand an effect of recuperation to ensue from the disjunction between two positions, that of an I represented in the text (who says he or she is unhappy) and that of the voice speaking the text. A reader's identification becomes split between the unhappy I represented by the text and another position situated outside the first I and at a critical distance from it. There the argument was framed mainly in terms of subjectivity but the effect can be analysed just as well in terms of language.

In the well-known passage in which he discusses the boy playing the so-called *fort/da* game, Freud suggests that an economy of loss and recompense may be one of the consequences of entering language. His question is how the 'repetition of this distressing experience' (loss of the mother) can be compensated for by the boy 'himself staging the disappearance and return' of something representing the mother. His answer is that the boy moves from passivity before the experience to actively doing something about it, repeating it, and so giving expression to the drive for mastery (*Bemächtigungstrieb*). Among other things, Freud says this psychic operation may account for how 'artistic play and artistic imitation carried out by adults, which unlike children's, are aimed at an audience, do not spare the spectators (for instance, in tragedy) the most painful experiences and can yet be felt by them as highly enjoyable'. On this showing representation itself, even the mere fact of linguistic representation without further dramatization, is enough to provide the statement of loss in language which also affords the reader a position in which to stand back from and to that extent master the loss. How men or women experience this effect will depend on their asymmetrical relation to mastery, an avowedly gendered term. As with melancholy, nostalgia and self-pity, the rhetoric of pathos is pleasurable when positive features in the speaking are introduced to make up for negative meanings in the statement.

A notable instance of Wordsworth's rhetoric of pathos comes in the ending of the 'Immortality' Ode, part of the last stanza of which runs as follows:

> The Clouds that gather round the setting sun
> Do take a sober colouring from an eye
> That hath kept watch o'er man's mortality;
> Another race hath been, and other palms are won.
> Thanks to the human heart by which we live,
> Thanks to its tenderness, its joys, and fears,
> To me the meanest flower that blows can give
> Thoughts that do often life too deep for tears.

Though obviously much less broad, the contrast between what is said and how it's said is just as it is in Shelley's poem on death. The speaker says that the individual life sinks below the horizon as surely as the sun sets in the west, that to watch is to watch people pass on, that human life is a flower which blooms only to fade, that we all die, that loss is constant, final and irremediable. But a certain use of intertextuality (Gray has a line on 'the meanest floweret of the vale' in 'Ode on the Pleasure arising from Vicissitude') , the dignified simplicity of a generalized vocabulary ('an eye,' 'the human heart', 'the meanest flower'), carefully sustained syntax, a metric running steadily and evenly across the formal repetitions, the perfectly pitched tone of voice firmly yet gently rising and falling – all converge in a controlled and sober rhetoric which offers to *know* and *master* any loss discussed.

Pathos, then, may be defined as a mechanism or trope in which loss admitted at the level of statement is to be redeemed at the level of utterance. This is a rhetoric much older than the poems of Wordsworth. There is the Old Testament:

> Yet man is born unto trouble,
> As the sparks fly upward . . .
> *(Job: v: 7)*

In the closing lines of Sophocles' play, *Oedipus the King*, the Chorus refer back to the fate of Oedipus in words which adapt a popular saying, first attributed to Solon:

> ὥστε θνητὸν ὄντ' ἐκείην τὴν τελευταίαν ἰδεῖν
> ἡμέραν ἐπισκοποῦντα μηδὲν ὀλβίςειν, πρὶν ἂν
> τέρμα τοῦ βίου περάσῃ μηδὲν ἀλγεινὸν παθών.
> ('so watching to see that last day call no mortal
> being happy until they have crossed the finishing-line
> of life without suffering pain.')
> *(II: 1528–30)*

In Virgil's *Aeneid*, when, after shipwreck, Aeneas enters Carthage and sees scenes on the walls of Juno's temple depicting the destruction of Troy, he declares that 'here too' (hic etiam):

> sunt lacrimae rerum et mentem mortalia tangunt
> ('there are tears for the sorrow of things and mortality touches the heart')
> *(I: 462)*

The line is imitated by Wordsworth in 'Laodamia':

> Yet tears to human suffering are due;
> And mortal hopes defeated and o'erthrown
> Are mourned by man . . .

In *The Divine Comedy* Cacciaguida foretells Dante's exile to him:

> Tu proverai sì come sa di sale
>   lo pane altrui, e com'è duro calle
>   lo scendere e il salir per l'altrui scale.
> ('You will find out how salty someone else's
>   bread tastes and how hard it is
>   to go up and down someone else's staircase.')
> *(Paradiso, xvii: 58–60)*

In Shakespeare the rhetoric of pathos is usually instanced from the last scene of *King Lear* but a less familiar example would be the scene towards the end of *Antony and Cleopatra* (IV. ii) when a group of soldiers on guard at night is mystified by music in the air and under the earth until one exclaims:

> 'Tis the god Hercules, whom Antony loved,
> Now leaves him.

An example from Tennyson might be the section of *In Memoriam* (xix) relating the death of Hallam to the strange ebb and flow of the River Severn (near which he was buried):

> The tide flows down, the wave again
>   Is vocal in its wooded walls;
>   My deeper anguish also falls,
> And I can speak a little then.

Lacan does suggest that human society is founded as a ritual act of mourning for loss though, rather than being seen as expression of some universal experience of nature, each of these different texts can be analysed as instances of a particular use of rhetoric.

Everything else being equal, the necessary condition for such rhetoric is understatement, or rather plain statement, a matter particularly of syntactical organization. Shelley's line from 'Ode to the West Wind':

> I fall upon the thorns of life! I bleed!

fails to qualify not so much because of the hysterical overstatement in its content as its refusal of a sustained syntax. At the other extreme, an over-embellished syntax, one which too obviously struggles for control of what's being said, implies not confidence and mastery but rather uncertainty, as perhaps in the final couplet of Shakespeare's 'Sonnet 129':

> All this the world well knows; yet none knows well
> To shun the heaven that leads men to this hell.

A measure of syntactical subordination and co-ordination, by attempting to achieve closure in the signifying chain, provides a position of relative fixity for the speaking subject. Repetition of stated loss, I suggest, would thus be mitigated and contained by a mastery provided in the means of representation.

Coleridge complained about what he called 'a *matter-of-factness*' in some of Wordsworth's poems. That feature contributes the effect of sincerity in many of them but it also helps to create the rhetoric of pathos, depending as it does on a balance between litotes and hyperbole, understatement and overstatement. Undoubtedly it is an effect Wordsworth can pull off

with great consistency, as for instance in the sonnet ('After-Thought')
which contrasts the ever-flowing River Duddon with human mortality:

> While we, the brave, the mighty, and the wise,
> We Men, who in our morn of youth defied
> The elements, must vanish; – be it so!
> Enough, if something from our hands have power
> To live, and act, and serve the future hour;
> And if, as toward the silent tomb we go,
> Through love, through hope, and faith's transcendent dower,
> We feel that we are greater than we know.

The simplicity of the abstract vocabulary ('love', 'hope', 'faith') helps
this, as possibly does a half-memory that this recalls Milton's line for a
created Adam, 'And feel that I am happier than I know' (*Paradise Lost*,
VIII: 282). Control over loss is especially written in by the syntactical
structure moving from the conditional ('if, as toward') across the repetitions ('Through love, through hope') and culminating in the comparative
('greater than').

Also Miltonic is Wordsworth's reworking of the sonnet in which
Milton dreams his dead wife has been returned to him ('Methought I saw
my late espoused Saint'). Wordsworth's sonnet, 'Surprised by joy', moves
on from the older tradition of dreams and visions to a more personal
psychology:

> Surprised by joy – impatient as the Wind
> I turned to share the transport – Oh! with whom
> But Thee, deep buried in the silent tomb . . .

Momentarily forgetting she was dead, the speaker turns to find the other
missing and so is reminded more intensely of her absence, a moment he
says is as bad as the one when she died:

> when I stood forlorn,
> Knowing my heart's best treasure was no more;
> That neither present time, nor years unborn
> Could to my sight that heavenly face restore.

Again the statement of loss is matched by control enforced through
the syntax and in the intonation: the triple negatives ('no more . . .',
'neither . . .', 'nor . . .') move towards climax in the positive assertion of
the last line, heavy pauses after 'time' and 'unborn' lead into the relatively
forceful yet even intonation extending along all of the final line.

There is a passage I've cited twice before, in different connections, but
am not reluctant to give once again, from *The Prelude* (XII: 272ff.):

> The days gone by
> Return upon me almost from the dawn

> Of life: the hiding places of man's power
> Open; I would approach them, but they close.
> I see by glimpses now; when age comes on,
> May scarcely see at all; and I would give,
> While yet we may, as far as words can give,
> Substance and life to what I feel . . .

This passage leans on the plangent cadences and subtle control of intonation made possible by playing off the iambic pentameter line-ending against sense and syntactical progression which Milton uses so effectively when he describes his blindness in *Paradise Lost*:

> Thus with the Year
> Seasons return, but not to mee returns
> Day, or the sweet approach of Ev'n or Morn,
> Or sight of vernal bloom, or Summers Rose,
> Or flocks, or herds, or human face divine . . .
>
> (*III: 40–44*)

Milton is concerned for the loss of physical sight and, with it, fuller pleasure in the external world and human company, Wordsworth with the loss of spiritual insight and certainty of his own importance. Yet the tones of mourning and pathos are closely comparable. We are discussing a rhetoric of pathos rather than pathos, words rather than feelings. Among other things, this is proven by how easy it is to show the derivation of a text, not from feelings, but from another text.

Since the general tendency of this book has been to urge that Wordsworth is to be seen as an effect, not a presence, it is appropriate to conclude this short chapter on language by recalling, emblematically, something about William Wordsworth and his compositional habits. According to Dorothy Wordsworth's journal (15 April 1802) William was with her when she saw the daffodils in the woods beyond Gowbarrow Park but he did not write about them until two years later and, so may have been influenced as much by her journal entry as by his own memory. He did meet the man claimed as original for the Leech-gatherer but the man was not on the moors but on a highway and not gathering leeches but begging. He met him with Dorothy (who does not appear in the poem) and again wrote up the experience two years after and with the benefit of Dorothy's text to hand (3 October 1800). If he did see the woman who becomes the Solitary Reaper in his tour of Scotland in 1803 he wrote about her two years later with the benefit of a manuscript by his friend, Thomas Wilkinson, of a Tour of Scotland from which he borrowed some phrases for the poem. As ever, 'it is the world of words that creates the world of things'.

8

The Heart of a Heartless World

τοῦ λόγου δέοντος ξυνοῦ ζώουσιν οἱ πολλοί
ὡς ἰδίαν ἔχοντες φρόνησιν.
('most people live as if they had their own
private way of thinking')

Heraclitus

Here is one of the 'Lucy' poems (it mentions a River Dove, of which there is more than one in the north of England):

> She dwelt among the untrodden ways
>   Beside the springs of Dove,
> A Maid whom there were none to praise
>   And very few to love:
>
> A violet by a mossy stone
>   Half hidden from the eye!
> – Fair as a star, when only one
>   Is shining in the sky.
>
> She lived unknown, and few could know
>   When Lucy ceased to be;
> But she is in her grave, and, oh,
>   The difference to me!

The first and third verses are in the past tense, in the third person and in sustained syntax – it's typical of writing. But this form of discourse gives way to another kind in the second stanza for this is in the present tense, in the first/second person of I/you address, and draws on the broken syntactic juxtapositions of speech rather than the subordinated syntax usual in written discourse. Between the first and last verse Lucy passes from life into death, from her out-of-the-way home to the grave, from little public knowledge to being known only – especially – to the speaker: this narrative represents a world in which there is temporal difference, spatial difference and the difference introduced by the Other whose recognition Lucy might win. Already, though, there are moves to exclude and surpass this narrative – what Wordsworth elsewhere writes off with casual contempt as 'the heavy and the weary weight / Of all this unintelligible world' – by pressing into another dimension beyond difference. Associated with an 'untrodden' way, outside social usage, Lucy is a Maid, that is, virgin, as unmixed and purely herself as the source ('springs') of the River Dove where she 'dwelt', like the Word which was made flesh and 'dwelt' among us in the first chapter of St John.

Thus anticipated, another domain interrupts the narrative and the text in the middle stanza. As an object for the speaker's subjectivity, Lucy so completely possesses the privilege of satisfying his needs that she fills the whole universe for him from microcosm – a violet by a stone – to macrocosm, where the planet Venus, because it is closest, is always the first to appear at night and last to disappear at dawn. She leaves no gap in his subjective demands. Implicitly addressed directly ['(You are) a Violet by . . .'], she is rendered through concrete objects rather than ideas, images whose unlikely juxtaposition (a small purple flower, a heavenly body) is a symptom of how powerfully and personally he imagines the tenseless present of his dyadic fulfilment in her.

'Like a Prayer' by Madonna was a hit across the English-speaking world in 1989, accompanied by a video which caused some controversy. In a Baroque church Madonna adores a black saint who miraculously comes to life. The words of a song are diminished without the music, but there are words nevertheless. In the video Madonna sings verses with muted choir and organ in the background, band accompaniment for the chorus, as follows:

> Life is a mystery –
> Everyone must stand alone.
> I hear you call my name –
> And it feels like home.
>
> *Chorus:*
> When you call my name
> It's like a little prayer.
> I'm down on my knees –
> I wanna take you there.
> In the midnight hour
> I can feel your power.

Just like a prayer
You know I'll take you there.

I hear your voice –
It's like an angel sighing.
I have no choice –
I hear your voice –
Feels like flying.
I close my eyes –
O God I think I'm falling
Out of the sky.
I close my eyes –
Heaven help me.

Chorus: When you call, etc.

Like a child
You whisper softly to me.
You're in control
Just like a child
Now I'm dancing –
It's like a dream.
No end and no beginning
You're here with me.
It's like a dream.
Let the choir sing.

Chorus: When you call etc.

Unlike the Wordsworth text, this is explicitly erotic. Like it, however, it begins by dismissing the world as unintelligible ('a mystery') and without communal purpose ('Everyone must stand alone'). From this meaningless Other the song flies as fast as it can into a transcendental alternative, though one which, for local reasons perhaps, is much more explicitly supernaturalized than in Wordsworth's secular humanism. Thereafter, the text aims to close itself off by taking as its 'home' an ecstatic dimension very like that envisioned in the middle of the 'Lucy' poem. Spatial difference vanishes into a kind of void or spacelessness defined only by 'flying' and 'falling', normal temporality is replaced by a separated moment ('the midnight hour'), and the only recognition acknowledged is that of total mutuality. Roles of domination and subordination are to correspond exactly, her answer to his call, her promise to take him there to his little prayer. In a similar syntax to that of Wordsworth – brief phrases juxtaposed without subordination – and in an identical I/you form of discourse the song dramatizes a sense of dyadic reciprocity in an apparently endless present, the only threat – her falling – apparently made good as a further degree of bliss. A dream is wished for,

the world of the child, pure presence without temporal or spatial difference ('No end and no beginning').

Wordsworth's poem is in regular quatrains, alternating lines of
four and three stresses, with a rhyme scheme *abab*. But what is said
refuses to admit dependence of the representation of an individual
voice on its representation – far from it, the text is contrived to simulate
the movement of a voice really speaking, interrupting itself with the
pressure of feeling at the interjection 'Fair as a star', mimicking a sob in
the throat with 'and, oh, / The difference to me!' A song, performed on
video, even more obviously relies on a means of representation, but,
exactly as in the 'Lucy' poem, what is said tries to make the representation part of and subordinate to the presence of the voice. The repetitions
of the chorus, like Wordsworth's rhymes, are not foregrounded as
manifest effects of the signifier, mere sound, but rather are to be taken
up into the experience as repetitions wrung out by feelings so intense
the words have to be said more than once. In both cases language is to
be wholly expressive, full speech, completely rendering a self which is
only itself.

Wordsworth our contemporary

As read here Wordsworth's poetry speaks of the commonality of our
privacy – what I most share with others is the desire to be different from
them. That contradiction at the centre of modernity has been noted by
many writers over the past century and a half. Frederick Engels, writing
in a famous passage in 1844, describes people walking along the streets
in Manchester as seeming to have nothing in common except the rule
of keeping to their own side of the pavement. The 'isolation of the
individual', so typical of modernity, is, he says,

> nowhere so shamelessly barefaced, so self-conscious as just here in the
> crowding of the great city. The dissolution of mankind into monads of
> which each one has a separate principle and a separate purpose, the
> world of atoms, is here carried out to its utmost extreme.

Raymond Williams at the end of *The Country and the City* updates this
judgement in terms of traffic. The modern car is 'private, enclosed, an
individual vehicle in a pressing and merely aggregated common flow';
while obeying 'certain underlying conventions of external control . . . we
pursue our ultimately separate ways but in a common mode'. Or as in
the song by The Police, after launching in a bottle a message to the world
about my loneliness, I look out and see:

A hundred million bottles
Washed up on the shore.

Wordsworth's most famous line is 'I wandered lonely as a cloud': was he among the very first to experience this special modern loneliness? Providing the ultimate rationale for the self-made man, Mr Wordsworth's defensive response to such unhappiness is, 'I am a rock, I am an island'.

Wordsworth, as Robert Langbaum says, establishes for us the very model of 'the self-creating, self-regarding identity'. Although his poetic language, mixing flat matter-of-factness with nebulous abstractions, forms an obstacle to our living into his writing, if that barrier can be passed we find ourselves disconcertingly at home. To maintain the sense of dialectic between Wordsworth then and now I have deliberately set his texts alongside the collective fantasies set out for us in contemporary popular culture, to show that Frank Sinatra regrets his lost self as deeply as Wordsworth. This exercise suggests how intimately Wordsworth's poetry mirrors our world. Despite the distantiating effect of the writing, we find ourselves implicated in these texts. How could we step aside from the mastering gaze directed at the Solitary Reaper when television constantly requires us to look through the same superior eyes as the role of the Other is reassuringly played out for us by starving babies in Ethiopia, gorillas and their human friends in Borneo, gang-warriors in East Los Angeles, AIDS victims visited by the Princess of Wales? How can men not be pulled into some identification with the speaker of the 'Lucy' poems when a whole series of Hollywood films from 'Psycho' through 'Chinatown' to 'Fatal Attraction' is equally motivated by the view that the only safe woman is a dead woman? What can I say about myself without falling into the rhetoric of full speech linked with the tones of pathos which recuperate its failure as nostalgia, mourning and self-pity?

Our continuity now with Wordsworth's then, the degree to which our narcissism is his narcissism, has been assured by the development in the West around 1800 of a would-be transcendental domain as a special, separate place to be inhabited by art, pleasure and the self. It was to be, as Marx said of Christianity amid the Belsen slums of Victorian England, the heart of a heartless world; or as *The Prelude* says, at least as I prefer to read it, after the failure of 1789, there is no alternative but to mourn the loss of meaningful collectivity as a way to give life meaning. Whether the contradiction is better explained in terms of the social or the subjective, the impossibility of its project – to be a self wholly without dependence on the Other – is most clearly and critically expressed in psychoanalytic terms.

Writing of the would-be autonomous I am, Lacan refers to 'the philosophical *cogito* at the centre of the mirage that renders modern man so sure of being himself even in his uncertainties about himself, and even in the mistrust he has learned to practise against the traps of self-love'. What Wordsworth's poetry so vividly exemplifies is the self's struggle to extricate itself from the defiles of the Other – to find a version of language which seems to belong only to itself, to address an Other almost identical with itself, to find itself reflected in an Other as much like itself as possible, to admit loss as a means of recuperating it, and so on and so on, at all events to be an 'I am' and not 'I will have been'. All of which leaves us, surely, on the edge of comedy. The tragic endeavour of *The Prelude* is rewritten as it has to be, two centuries later, in the agonizing farce of Beckett's *The Unnameable*. Yet the rhetoric and contingencies of Wordsworth's then is written for us in language which can speak to us directly if, as we're invited, we take it over and perform it for ourselves and our own purposes.

Notes

Wordsworth criticism can be summarized under six headings:

1   *Collaborative.* This assumes very much the same things about the power of 'Imagination' and the reality of external 'Nature' as did Wordsworth, and then endlessly recycles the same autobiographical details alongside the poems and other contemporary texts, especially Coleridge but also Hazlitt and De Quincey. In very much this spirit Paul Hamilton [*Wordsworth* (Brighton: Harvester, 1986, p. 5)] asserts that 'Wordsworth's poetic contains its own theory' (like a sardine tin with the key inside).

2   *Celebrative.* Represented first by Harold Bloom in 1961 with *Visionary Company: A Reading of English Romantic Poetry* (New York: Doubleday) this has been set out, most importantly, by Geoffrey Hartman in *Wordsworth's Poetry 1787–1814* (New Haven, Conn.: Yale University Press, 1964). When Blake annotated Wordsworth's poems in 1826 he took a view consistent with his own position that 'One Power alone makes a Poet: Imagination, The Divine Vision' and criticized Wordsworthian submission to Nature as a bad thing [*Complete Writings of William Blake*, edited by Geoffrey Keynes (Oxford: Oxford University Press, 1966, p. 782)]; the American poet, Wallace Stevens, similarly affirmed that the mind must make its own world. Hartman follows both in arguing that 'by 1798' Wordsworth 'had come to firm self-consciousness and separated his imagination from nature' (p. 175); crucial to this reading is the passage from *The Prelude* (VI: 516–687) in which Wordsworth praises 'Imagination' as apparently self-creating, 'an unfathered vapour' (a passage to which Paul de Man had drawn particular attention in an essay of 1960; see *Deconstructive* criticism below). It may be noted that Hartman's 'Imagination' expresses itself in a dyadic relation between subject and object so that everything goes on just as before. And if, as I would assume, the self can become conscious of itself only as an effect of its reflection in the Other, one must ask how this supposedly autonomous and unfathered self-consciousness could lift itself by its own shoelaces? Hartman's move here (hardly his fault for it is structurally necessary to conventional literary criticism) is to invent a transcendental subject, 'Wordsworth', who stands outside the poems so that they are merely variable expressions of himself (see the way Hartman tamely reproduces the idea of 'the poem itself' in the passage I've cited in another connection; pp. 39–40). And the speaker of the poems – their speaking

voice – is not some imaginary 'Wordsworth' but the reader in the present. Hartman is nevertheless a strong critic whose reading currently prevails in much Wordsworth criticism; my book hopes to be one small text which intervenes to oppose that domination.

3 *Epistemological.* Chronologically parallel to Hartman's influence, there was the phenomenological or epistemological account of Wordsworth arising on the basis of a Kantian aesthetic. This was practised by René Wellek [e.g. 'Romanticism Reconsidered', in Northrop Frye (ed.) *Romanticism Reconsidered* (New York: Columbia University Press, 1963, pp. 107–133)] and by Earl Wasserman [e.g. 'The English Romanticism: The Grounds of Knowledge, *Studies in Romanticism*, vol. 4, No. 1, Autumn 1964, pp. 17–34], and anticipated somewhat earlier by M.H. Abrams in *The Mirror and the Lamp: Romantic Theory and the Critical Tradition* (Oxford: Oxford University Press, 1953) if not in 1949 in W.K. Wimsatt's essay on 'The Structure of Romantic Nature Imagery', reprinted in *The Verbal Icon* (London: Routledge, 1970).

4 *Deconstructive.* Such discussion begins with the essays written by Paul de Man between 1960 and 1979, and collected as part of *The Rhetoric of Romanticism* (New York: Columbia University Press, 1984). De Man, more powerfully and consistently than any before, makes the argument that subject/object unity is impossible. In a 1960 essay translated as 'Intentional Structure of the Romantic Image' he anticipates much of Hartman's position, drawing from the passage in Book VI of *The Prelude* on Imagination to assert that 'it makes a possibility for consciousness to exist entirely by and for itself, independently of all relationship with the outside world' (p. 16). De Man also introduces into Wordsworth criticism the claim that autobiography is impossible because it is always a 'manifestation . . . of a linguistic structure, (p. 71). Another crucial essay by de Man, taking up Walter Benjamin's distinction between symbol and allegory, is first published in 1969 as 'The Rhetoric of Temporality' and reprinted in the second edition of *Blindness and Insight* (London: Routledge, 1983). The essay reflects on subject/object unity, the nature of Romantic language, two 'selves' in Romantic poetry.

Coleridge distinguishes between allegory, in which characters and events are known by the reader to stand for certain general ideas (a young woman might represent Peace, for example) and a symbol, which 'partakes of the reality which it renders intelligible' [*The Statesman's Manual*, in W.G.T. Shedd, *Complete Works*, 7 Vols (New York: Harper, 1954, vol. 1, p. 438)]. De Man argues that valorization of the symbol at the expense of allegory depends on an aesthetics which 'refuses to distinguish between experience and the representation of experience' (p. 188) and the assumption that the symbol is 'part of the totality that it represents' (p. 191). This is impossible, de Man affirms, for two related reasons: the signifier (representation) cannot coincide with a signified (represented), nor subject with object (Romantic poetry is in fact allegorical in depending necessarily on the inherently *arbitrary* relation between signifier and signified such that meaning is always temporally deferred and never actually present). Romanticism is characterized both by the absence of a unified dialectic between subject and object, and its attempt to efface this lack, and this division issues in two selves related by ironic language: 'an empirical self that exists in a state of inauthenticity', deprived, that is, of subject/object unity; and 'a self that exists only in the form of a language that asserts the knowledge of this inauthenticity' (p. 214), a self-conscious self.

I shall attempt to counter this penetrating analysis by rethinking these two selves in terms of the represented I and the I speaking (subject of enounced and subject of enunciation), and will refer back to de Man's account at the appropriate junctures. But it is worth stating in advance what I consider the fatal flaw in his view. Failing to recognize that the text offers a position to its reader, de Man is able to treat both 'selves' as somehow *internal* to the text and part of it. In doing so he recuperates the effect of the reader's positioning by the text by means of the usual critical trope (identifying text with reader by assimilating both to the notion of the transcendental Author). While giving an incisive critique of the possibility that subject and object might mirror each other, de Man (his writing) cherishes his image reflected from the poetic text as 'Wordsworth'.

5 *Marxist.* Developing out of work by E.P. Thompson on the historical period in *The Making of the English Working Class* (London: Gollancz, 1963) and by Raymond Williams in *The Country and the City* (London: Chatto and Windus, 1973), Marxist and Left criticism includes David Simpson's *Wordsworth's Historical Imagination* (New York: Routledge, 1987), John Williams's *Wordsworth: Romantic Poetry and Revolutionary Politics* (Manchester: Manchester University Press, 1989) and Michael H. Friedman's *The Making of a Tory Humanist: William Wordsworth and the Idea of Community* (New York: Columbia University Press, 1979). Drawing equally on Marx and Freud Friedman argues that Wordsworth first sought fulfilment for himself in the community of the French Revolution but, checked by Oedipal guilt for his rebelliousness, gave this up in order to renew his identity among the 'perfect Republic of Shepherds and Agriculturalists' he found – or thought he found – in contemporary Westmoreland (Wordsworth writing in 1809, cited by Friedman in *The Making of a Tory Humanist*, p. 195). Marx and Freud, history and the unconscious, are supposedly held together merely as means, once again, to get at the 'real' Wordsworth who, in a wholly traditional manner, nestles inside *The Prelude*, Wordsworth's prose, the usual biographical texts, other historical texts.

Within this tradition Jerome McGann in *The Romantic Ideology: A Critical Investigation* (Chicago, Ill.: Chicago University Press, 1983) develops an account of Wordsworth in terms of a definition of Romantic ideology as denying its own historical origins, a definition therefore which follows in the wake of Pierre Macherey's *A Theory of Literary Production* (London: Routledge, 1978). Marjorie Levinson's *Wordsworth's Great Period Poems: Four Essays* (Cambridge: Cambridge University Press, 1986) represents a very provocative Machereyan attempt to make what is unspoken and contradictory in the poetic texts reveal meanings only analysable through recourse to History so that, as she writes, 'a manifold of contemporary meanings originally associated with or systematically informing the poet's representation, is restored to a work which defines by its illogical affirmation the contours of that repressed material' (p. 11). So a long account of what was happening in and around Tintern Abbey in the 1790s leads to the accurate but not unsurprising conclusion that in the 'Tintern Abbey' poem 'the primary poetic action is the suppression of the social' (p. 37).

Two reservations can be entered against this determination in both Friedman and Levinson to found the critique of the poetry in a historical narrative outside the text [as does Alan Liu's Machereyan study, *Wordsworth: The Sense of History* (Stanford, Calif.: Stanford University Press, 1989)] One is that it has the consequence of locking the poetry away from us in the history of its own time, leaving unanswered the question of what Wordsworth's poetry means for us now and why we, in the 1990s, should be reading it at all. Another is that you may not need to do this. Mary Jacobus [*Romanticism, Writing and Sexual Difference: Essays on 'The Prelude'* (Oxford: Clarendon Press, 1989, esp. pp. 69–93)] argues persuasively that since *The Prelude* is 'the text of history' (p. 70) it can now be read as itself a historical effect; in other words, that the historical referent appears *in* the text, albeit in a repressed form.

6 *Gender.* In a path-breaking essay first published in 1981, 'Sex and History in *The Prelude* (1805): Books Nine to Thirteen' [reprinted in *In Other Worlds* (New York: Routledge, 1987, pp. 46–76)], Gayatri Spivak proposes to read the gender implications of *The Prelude* on the basis of the Julia and Vaudracour story: 'Suppression of Julia, unemphatic retention of Vaudracour as sustained and negative condition of possibility of disavowal, his sublation into Coleridge, rememorating through the mediation of the figure of Dorothy his own Oedipal accession to the Law, Imagination as the androgyny of Nature and Man – Woman shut out' (pp. 56–7). In a paper of 1981, 'The Romantic Construction of the Unconscious' [in Francis Barker (ed.), *Literature, Politics and Theory* (London: Routledge, 1986, pp. 57–76)], Catherine Belsey argues that 'The project of *The Prelude* is both to sustain and finally to eliminate difference' (p. 73) and so, by consequence, sexual difference.

A number of essays in *Romanticism and Feminism*, edited by Ann K. Mellor (Indiana: Indiana University Press, 1988), reflect on Wordsworth's politics of gender, especially 'Troping Masculine Power in the Crisis of Poetic Identity' by Marlon B. Ross (pp. 26–51), an essay which follows through the phallocentrism of many Romantic writers, including Wordsworth's sense of 'power' [Ross has since expanded the essay in *The Contours of Masculine Desire* (New York: Oxford University Press, 1990)]. Mary Jacobus in *Romanticism, Writing and Sexual Difference* also develops an account of Wordsworth and gender in terms of a masculinity which seeks always to presents itself as phallogocentric and so must deny femininity and difference. Of women in *The Prelude* Jacobus says, 'Far from being emblems of sexual difference, they function precisely as defences against it' (p. 208); in a splitting of the ego, Wordsworth adheres to the image of a fetishized man in order to discard and disparage woman, thus maintaining a sense of unfallen self at the cost of a fallen one.

What I refer to in my 'Preface' as 'a degree of consensus' around the new paradigm in its application to Wordsworth's poetry is represented not only by de Man and the essays of J. Hillis Miller but also by the writing of Gayatri Spivak, Catherine Belsey, Robert Young, Mary Jacobus, and Keith Hanley (this and essays by Hillis Miller will be noted along the way). I have also leaned on psychoanalytic criticism, including Richard Onorato, *The Character of the Poet: Wordsworth in 'The Prelude'* (Princeton, NJ: Princeton University Press, 1971), and David Ellis, *Wordsworth, Freud and the Spots of Time* (Cambridge: Cambridge University Press, 1985).

Preface

page

xiii   'We ought to impute . . .'
W.K. Wimsatt and Monroe Beardsley, *The Verbal Icon* (London: Routledge, 1970), p. 5.

xiv   'his writing . . .'
J. Hillis Miller, 'On Edge: The Crossways of Contemporary Criticism', in Morris Eaves and Michael Fischer (eds), *Romanticism and Contemporary Criticism* (Ithaca, NY: Cornell University Press, 1986), pp. 96–126, p. 106.

xv   you have to rely . . . on a historical narrative
Even Marjorie Levinson, in her less than conventional version of Wordsworth, *Wordsworth's Great Period Poems*, locates his writing firmly in the period around 1800, and so at a point within a defined historical narrative.

xvi   'seductive instruction'
Levinson, ibid., p. 10.

1   Nature and Imagination

2   MS. JJ
For this, see William Wordsworth, *The Prelude 1799, 1805, 1850*, edited by Jonathan Wordsworth, M.H. Abrams and Stephen Gill (New York: Norton, 1979) (Norton Critical Editions), p. 492.

'running wild'
Samuel Taylor Coleridge, *Collected Letters of Samuel Taylor Coleridge*, edited by E.L. Griggs, 6 vols. (Oxford: Oxford University Press, 1956), vol. 1, p. 453.

the event and his perceptions
There are other ways of appropriating the real (astronomy, for example, or sub-atomic physics) than that made available by everyday human perception. And, further, it is only for the sake of clarity of exposition that I'm drawing the line here between perception and experience. In fact, perceptions are themselves already shaped for us by our knowledge and experience, as cognitive psychology amply shows. So the line could also be drawn between the real and perception or between experience and interpretation. We inherit a Cartesian tendency to pose the question in terms of a binary opposition; we really need a more imbricated sense of different overlapping layers between nature and culture, body and mind (more like the lovely epistemology which Statius narrates in 'Purgatorio' XXV of Dante's *Divine Comedy*). Obviously the real does enter Wordsworth's poetry to some degree – it would be harder to write like this if you lived in the Amazonian rainforest (what's left of it) than in the Lake District with its valleys and peaks so conveniently reared and moulded for the usual contrasting gender roles.

4   'It is not how things are . . .'
L.J.J. Wittgenstein, *Tractatus Logico-Philosophicus*, translated by D.F. Pears and B.F. McGuinness (London: Routledge and Kegan Paul, 1961), no. 6.44, p. 149.

'Why are there essents . . .'
Martin Heidegger, *An Introduction to Metaphysics*, translated by Ralph Manheim (New Haven, CT: Yale University Press, 1959), p. 1.

'Then sometimes . . .'
Paul de Man in 1960 in 'Intentional Structure of the Romantic Image' made the 'Boy of Winander' passage crucial to his convincing argument that Wordsworth is not a poet of plenitude and the union between subject and object but rather one who, recognizing the actual absence of such a union, wishes the more to find it. Instead of standing and listening to the owls, de Man stresses, the boy 'hung' there, in some anxiety and so in some awareness of 'loss of the sense of correspondence' between subject and object (*The Rhetoric of Romanticism*, p. 53). The context of the passage in *The Prelude* must also affect the reading, appearing as it does after the dream of the Shell and the Stone (V: 50–140) and before the story of the man found drowned (426–59). This has provoked Cynthia Chase to point out that it is 'as if the Boy, suspended in the silence, were "received / Into the bosom of the steady lake"' [*Decomposing Figures: Rhetorical Readings in the Romantic Tradition* (Baltimore, MA: Johns Hopkins University Press, 1986), p. 17]. Jonathan Arac has considered the revisions made to the passage, see 'Bounding Lines: *The Prelude* and Critical Revision', in *Post-Structuralist Readings of English Poetry*, edited by Richard Machin and Christopher Norris (Cambridge: Cambridge University Press, 1987), pp. 227–47. I would still emphasize

the silence of the owls which so aptly opens onto the possibilities of both absence and plenitude (and I have undoubtedly exploited this in my invented examples).

6   'romantic wit'
Wimsatt, *The Verbal Icon*, p. 109.

'This expression, "far" . . .'
Thomas De Quincey, *Recollections of the Lakes and the Lake Poets* (Harmondsworth: Penguin, 1970), p. 161.

to lure Nature as the other
It would be easy to write a book on Lacan's distinction between the Big Other and the small other. It will have to suffice here to say that the Other is everything except me while the other is, as it were, my other, a point I have won for myself from the Other.

Empiricism can be defined . . .
For an excellent introduction, see Stephen Priest, *The British Empiricists* (Harmondsworth: Penguin, 1990).

7   'generally involves knowledge . . .'
R.L. Gregory, *Eye and Brain: The Psychology of Seeing*, 3rd edn (London: Weidenfield and Nicolson, 1977), p. 10.

'the symbol manifests . . .'
Jacques Lacan, *Ecrits: A Selection*, translated by Alan Sheridan (London: Tavistock, 1977), p. 104.

'Hunger is hunger'
Karl Marx, 'Introduction', *Grundrisse* (Harmondsworth: Penguin, 1973), p. 92.

8   'Wordsworth's "Nature"'
Christopher Caudwell, *Illusion and Reality, A Study of the Sources of Poetry*, (London: Lawrence and Wishart, 1946), p. 93.

'solidarity between the human spirit and the world'
See Alain Robbe-Grillet, 'Old "Values" and the New Novel (Nature, Humanism, Tragedy)', translated by Bruce Morrissette, *Evergreen Review*, vol. 9, no. 9 (Summer 1959), pp. 98–118, p. 99 (originally published in *Nouvelle Nouvelle Revue Française*, no. 70 (October 1958), pp. 580–604.

'things are things, and man is only man'
Ibid., p. 100. I have marked this with *sic*, the first occasion in my text at which a cited text uses a masculine noun or pronoun to comprehend men and women. I will not note subsequent examples.

'a village "crouching"'
Ibid., p. 101.

'record the separation'
Ibid., p. 116.

9   'the poet . . . nothing affirms'
Philip Sidney, 'An Apology for Poetry', in Edmund D. Jones (ed.), *English Critical Essays (Sixteenth, Seventeenth and Eighteenth Centuries* (Oxford: Oxford University Press, 1947), p. 33.

12   the rational values of his society
For Nature in Pope and Wordsworth, see Basil Willey, *The Eighteenth-Century Background* (Harmondsworth: Penguin, 1962).

14   'You shall not . . .'
William Blake, 'Annotations to "The Excursion"', *The Complete Writings*, p. 784.

16   a transition from demand to desire
See Lacan, *Ecrits*, pp. 286–7.

'What is meant . . .'
A.H. Clough, *Poems and Prose Remains* (London, 1869, p. 319) cited by Robert Young, '"For Thou Wert There": History, Erasure, and Superscription in The Prelude,', *Demarcating the Disciplines*, Glyph Textual Studies (new series), vol. 1 (Minneapolis: University of Minnesota Press, 1986), pp. 103–128, p. 107.

2 Romantic Ideology

18   'Between 1793 and . . .'
Jerome McGann, *The Romantic Ideology* (Chicago, ILL: University of Chicago Press, 1983), p. 88.

'The common feat . . .'
Wimsatt, *The Verbal Icon*, p. 110.

'What is distinctive . . .'
Abrams, *The Mirror and the Lamp*, p. 64.

'that attempt . . .'
Wellek, *Romanticism Reconsidered*, p. 133.

This demand for unity between subject and object
In her brilliant and suggestive essay Catherine Belsey explores the effect of this transcendental unity as Wordsworth produces it in the 'Boating' passage from *The Prelude*; see *Literature, Politics and Theory*, pp. 57–76.

the Renaissance
In *The Discovery of the Individual, 1050–1200* (London: SPCK, 1972), Colin Morris argues that properly we should speak of 'the Renaissance of the twelfth century' (p. 7).

19   'not only creates . . .'
Marx, *Grundrisse*, p. 92.

the Hungarian Marxist
Georg Lukács, *History and Class Consciousness*, translated by Rodney
Livingston (London: Lawrence and Wishart, 1971), esp. pp. 83–140.

20   Romantic ideology as a response
A major empirical objection to his account of Romantic ideology would
be that by the 1790s even in England the industrialisation had only
affected tiny enclaves in the economy, as Steve Rigby points out in
Engels and the Formation of Marxism: History, Dialectics and Revolution
(Manchester: Manchester University Press, 1992), pp. 59–63.

'the repository of all . . .'
Lukács, *History and Class Consciousness*, p. 136.

never previously carried
See Terry Eagleton, *The Ideology of the Aesthetic* (Oxford: Blackwell,
1990).

Christopher Caudwell . . . Raymond Williams
Caudwell in *Illusion and Reality*, Raymond Williams in *The Country and
the City*, esp. Ch. 13, 'The Green Language'.

'productive force determinism'
For a critique of Marxism (though not of Lukács) along these lines, see
Steve Rigby, *Marxism and History: A Critical Introduction* (Manchester:
Manchester University Press, 1987).

21   some sense of his or her own identity
In *History, Labour, and Freedom: Themes from Marx* (Oxford: Clarendon
Press, 1985, esp. pp. 136–54), G.A. Cohen argues against classic Marxism
that 'nothing is more essentially human' than 'the need for self identity'
(p. 154).

in outline . . . the typical eighteenth-century village
This is almost exactly the picture Wordsworth paints of the way a rural
community of independent yeoman farmers in Cumbria has been
destroyed in his own lifetime.

22   'What we are faced with . . .'
Lacan, *Ecrits*, pp. 26–7.

'It was the . . .'
Georg Lukács, *The Historical Novel*, translated by Hannah and Stanley
Mitchell (London: Merlin, 1962), p. 23.

24   'For a multitude of causes . . .'
'Preface' to *Lyrical Ballads*, *The Poetical Works of William Wordsworth*,

edited by Ernest de Selincourt and Helen Darbishire, 5 vols, reprinted (Oxford: Oxford University Press, 1952–59), vol. 2, p. 389.

26   deeply wonderful personal experiences
Geoffrey Hartman, for instance, for whom Wordsworth's work represents ever-increasing acts of self-consciousness, takes it that the importance for Wordsworth is that he begins to recognize in his experience of the Revolution 'the apocalyptic implication of his break with nature', *Wordsworth's Poetry, 1787–1814*, p. 243.

The first and second books
All quotations will be from the first published edition of the poem as it appeared after the death of the historical author in 1850.

27   endeavours to interpret this dream
The reader who wishes to pursue these can pick up the trail with the chapter on it in J. Hillis Miller, *The Linguistic Moment: From Wordsworth to Stevens* (Princeton, NJ: Princeton University Press 1985), pp. 78–113.

'tired of London'
Boswell's Life of Johnson, edited by C.G. Osgood (New York: Scribner's, 1917), p. 341.

28   'a failure of identity'
Williams, *The Country and the City*, p. 186.

'progression, not a break'
Robert Young, '"For Thou Wert There": History, Erasure and Superscription in The Prelude', p. 114. Young goes on to propose that in Wordsworth's personal experience 'private and public' are not divided (p. 112).

3 The Wordsworth Experience

35   'a speaking voice' . . . 'the "I" represented'
The terms correspond to Jacques Lacan's distinction between the subject of the enunciation and the subject of the enounced (or statement): see Roman Jakobson, 'Shifters, verbal categories, and the Russian verb' (1957) in *Word and Language* (The Hague: Mouton, 1971), pp. 133–4; and Jacques Lacan, *Four Fundamental Concepts of Psycho-Analysis*, translated by Alan Sheridan (London: Hogarth, 1977), p. 139. I have also discussed the difference in relation to poetry in *Poetry as Discourse* (London: Routledge, 1983), pp. 40–47. See also the discussion in Chapter 5, pp. 78–81.

'Lines – Composed a few miles above Tintern Abbey, on revisiting the banks of the Wye during a tour. July 13, 1798'
It is a harmless and almost irresistible game to imagine what William

Wordsworth, historical author, did or did not see when he wrote a poem tendentiously entitled as above. As part of writing this book, your humble author dutifully visited Tintern Abbey on 23 September 1991 and was struck by a number of questions. Since the River Wye, which flows past the abbey, is tidal, how far upstream of the ruins do you have to go before you hear the waters 'rolling from their mountain springs'? And how close to the river? Since the valley of the Wye is V-shaped and wooded above Tintern, where do you see 'steep and lofty cliffs'? There are some downstream of Tintern but the titling says 'above'. Where is there 'a sounding cataract'? There are plenty in the Lake District, none I could see or hear near Tintern. How many miles above Tintern Abbey is Wordsworth supposed to be, since a sharp bend in the river conceals the abbey a mile or so upstream?

The abbey was founded by the Cistercians in 1311 and at its peak had about 440 monks worshippinq and living communally there. Few were left when Henry VIII's campaign to break the power of the Catholic Church in England forced it to be surrendered to the King on 3 September 1536. The lead from the roof was sold off to a member of the local gentry and, open to the sky, the great buildings soon fell to pieces leaving 'Bare ruined choirs where late the sweet birds sang'. The mother house of the Cistercians as Citeaux had been suppressed by the Revolutionary powers in 1790. Marjorie Levinson (*Wordsworth's Great Period Poems*) includes some fascinating material on what was happening around the abbey in the 1790s and stresses that Wordsworth in 1798 would associate its destruction with the attack on the convent of Chartreuse mentioned in *The Prelude* (VI: 375–488). Perhaps; but I find it just as likely Wordsworth was thinking of a parallel between what Henry VIII did to the abbey in 1536 and what the Revolution did to other Cistercian monasteries in 1790. In any case, as David Robinson points out in an excellent guide, *William Wordsworth's Tintern* (Cadw: Welsh Historical Monuments, 1991): 'Neither Tintern Abbey nor even the sylvan Wye is the subject of the poem. Wordsworth himself is' (p. 4).

39   'I have remarked . . .'
De Quincey, *Recollections of the Lakes and Lake Poets*, p. 160.

'the effect was . . .'
Onorato, *The Character of the Poet: Wordsworth in 'The Prelude'*, p. 187.

'A definition . . .'
Hartman, *Wordsworth's Poetry*, pp. 17–18.

41   '"Nature" is not . . .'
Martin Heidegger, *Being and Time*, translated by John Macquarrie and Edward Robinson (Oxford: Blackwell, 1962), p. 100.

Keith Hanley
In a series of important and suggestive essays Hanley has made this Freud

paper crucial to his reading of Wordsworth's life; see 'Describing the Revolution: Wordsworth, Freud and Lacan', *Tropes of Revolution*, edited by C.C. Barfoot and Theo D'haen (Amsterdam: Rhodopi, 1991), pp. 90–113; '"A Poet's History": Wordsworth and Revolutionary Discourse', in Pauline Fletcher and John Murphy (eds), *Wordsworth in Context*, Bucknell Review Series vol. xxxvi, no. 1 (Lewisburg: Bucknell University Press, 1992), pp. 35–66; 'Crossings Out: The Problem of Textual Passage in *The Prelude*', in Robert Brinkley and Keith Hanley (eds), *Romantic Revisions* (Cambridge: Cambridge University Press, 1992), pp. 103–135.

42   'by the evidence . . .'
Freud, 'A Disturbance of Memory on the Acropolis', *Penguin Freud Library* (Harmondsworth: Penguin, 1974–86) (hereafter *PFL*), vol. 11, pp. 447–56, p. 452.

the uncanny
See Freud, 'The Uncanny', *PFL* vol. 14, pp. 335–77.

'I walk back . . .'
Roland Barthes, *A Lover's Discourse: Fragments* (Harmondsworth: Penguin, 1990), pp. 87–8.

43   'Nothing was more difficult . . .'
Wordsworth to Mrs Fenwick, 1843, *The Poetical Works*, vol. 4, p. 463 (note appended to 'Immortality' Ode). *The Prelude* gives a version of the same experience as:

> . . . what I saw
> Appeared like something in myself, a dream,
> A prospect in the mind.
>   (*II: 350–2*)

44   The identity of the ego must be secured . . . as a position in – and across – time.
Though Paul de Man's 1969 essay, 'The Rhetoric of Temporality', was not written under the influence of Lacan, he nevertheless regards the relationship between subject and object in Romanticism as 'a relationship of the subject toward itself', that by this means the self aims 'to borrow, so to speak, the temporal stability that it lacks from nature'; *Blindness and Insight*, p. 196, 197.

45   feral children
See Paul Q. Hirst and Penny Woolley, *Social Relations and Human Attributes* (London: Macmillan, 1982), pp. 44–60; *The Guardian* (28 August 1987) reported a girl, Wang Xianfeng, from Liaoning Province in China, who was brought up by pigs until she was 10: 'While an infant, she was left to live with the family of pigs, sucking pig milk, crawling like a pig and imitating pig behaviour'. After 3 years' special training she returned to normal life.

'the ego has to be developed'
Freud, 'On Narcissism: An Introduction', *PFL*, vol. 11, p. 69.

46 the Lacanian account
See *Ecrits*, pp. 1–7.

'What does one experience . . .'
Jean-Jacques Rousseau, 'Les Réveries du promeneur solitaire', *Oeuvres Complètes*, edition La Pléiade, 4 vols (Paris: Gallimard, 1959), vol. 1, p. 1047.

50 'is written for . . .'
James Agee and Walker Evans, *Let Us Now Praise Famous Men* (London: Peter Owen, 1965), p. 14.

51 'A Highland Woman'
Sorley Maclean, *Spring Tide and Neap Tide: Selected Poems 1932–72* (Edinburgh: Canongate, 1977); the poems are also presented in Gaelic.

4 Autobiography 1: Theme

54 'Information and events . . .'
Elizabeth Bruss, *Autobiographical Acts* (Baltimore, MD: Johns Hopkins University Press, 1976), p. 7; see also Robert Elbaz, *The Changing Nature of the Self: A Critical Study of the Autobiographic Discourse* (London: Croom Helm, 1988); 'Autobiography and Truth', in David Ellis, *Wordsworth, Freud and Spots of Time*, pp. 167–78; and of course Paul de Man, 'Autobiography as De-Facement', in *The Rhetoric of Romanticism*, pp. 67–81.

'The monumental writing . . .'
Jonathan Wordsworth, *William Wordsworth: The Borders of Vision* (Oxford: Oxford University Press, 1983), p. 57.

55 'the autobiographer . . .'
Elbaz, *Changing Nature of the Self*, p. 16.

'This is only a dream'
See Freud, *The Interpretation of Dreams*, *PFL*, vol. 5, pp. 453, 628–9. I would suspect that Lord Russell's absolutely documentary account of the Holocaust, *The Scourge of the Swastika*, became a bestseller partly because its truth-claims made possible certain sado-masochistic fantasies; the journal of Amnesty International, a cause it is impossible not to support, makes harrowing reading, and I know some people who buy the journal but won't read it.

56 'For it being . . .'
John Locke, *An Essay Concerning Human Understanding*, edited by Peter

Nidditch (Oxford: Clarendon Press, 1975), Book 2, Ch. 27, s. 10, p. 336.

57   'I admit that . . .'
Freud, *PFL*, vol. 9, p. 344 fn; the implication of deferred interpretation has been brought out by Jacques Derrida in 'Freud and the Scene of Writing', *Writing and Difference* (London: Routledge, 1978), pp. 196–231.

58   'the true practical general law . . .'
Coleridge, *Biographia Literaria*, 2 vols edited by John Shawcross (Oxford: Oxford University Press, 1949), vol. 1, p. 87.

60   the traditional Western conception . . . of time
This description is justified for reasons I have tried to give in 'Appendix 1: Time and Different Times', in *Literary into Cultural Studies* (London: Routledge, 1991), pp. 182–88.

62   'It seems that . . .'
Cited by Freud, *Leonardo da Vinci and a Memory of his Childhood* (1910), *PFL*, vol. 14 (Harmondsworth: Penguin, 1985), p. 172. As every school-girl knows, Freud was misled by a bad German translation and it wasn't a vulture but a kite.

63   *screen memories*
These are mentioned by several critics of Wordsworth but I have not seen the idea adequately developed; see Onorato, *The Character of the Poet*, pp. 208–211, p. 252; David Ellis, *Wordsworth, Freud and the Spots of Time*, pp. 18–19, 63, 66; Michael H. Friedman, *The Making of a Tory Humanist*, p. 18; Mary Jacobus, *Romanticism, Writing and Sexual Difference*, p. 15. Freud's paper on 'Screen Memories' is not in the *Penguin Freud Library* but can be found in the *Standard Edition*, edited by John Strachey, vol. III, pp. 301–322, though there are other similar discussions in *The Psychopathology of Everyday Life*, *PFL*, vol. 5, pp. 83–92 and in *Introductory Lectures*, *PFL*, vol. 1, pp. 235–8, and 'Remembering, Repeating and Working Through', *Standard Edition*, vol. 12, pp. 145–156.

the uncanny
See Freud's paper of this name, *PFL*, vol. 14, pp. 336–76.

64   his father died
Hamlet describes how his mother 'followed my poor father's body' and Wordsworth writes how he 'followed his [father's] body to the grave', and, as has been pointed out, 'such indisputable shapes' as Wordsworth sees (I: 324) may recall Hamlet's worry that his father's ghost should appear in 'such a questionable shape'.

66   'Wordsworth frankly . . .'
William Empson, *Seven Types of Ambiguity* (London: Chatto and Windus, 1930), p. 20.

67   'I remember my mother . . .'
From the 'Autobiographical Memoranda' William Wordsworth dictated
a few years before his death, *The Prose Works of William Wordsworth*, 3
vols edited by W.J.B. Owen and J.M. Smyser (Oxford: Clarendon Press,
1974), vol. 3, p. 371.

68   'landscapes . . . are invariably . . .'
The whole passage from Freud touches directly on Wordsworth and
contains one of his driest jokes – 'In some dreams of landscapes or other
localities emphasis is laid in the dream itself on a convinced feeling of
having been there once before. (Occurrences of *déjà-vu* in dreams have
a special meaning.) These places are invariably the genitals of the
dreamer's mother; there is indeed no other place about which one can
assert with such conviction that one has been there once before.' *Interpretation of Dreams*, *PFL*, vol. 4, p. 524.

5   Autobiography 2: Rhetoric

70   *Hysterics suffer . . .*
Josef Breuer and Sigmund Freud, *Studies on Hysteria*, *PFL*, vol. 3,
p. 58.

'the lyrics of every song', 'I had found'
Bob Geldof, *Is That It?*, with Paul Vallely (Harmondsworth: Penguin,
1986), pp. 23, 134.

71   'full speech'
Lacan, *Ecrits*, p. 48. Full speech is what the analyst has to work on for
it is 'full speech in so far as it realises the truth of the subject': *The
Seminar of Jacques Lacan: Book I, Freud's Papers on Technique 1953–1954*,
translated by John Forrester (Cambridge: Cambridge University Press,
1988), p. 50. Derrida has another, narrower version of full speech,
defining it only by saying 'there is no full speech' and referring to the
impossibility 'that a sign, the unity of a signifier and a signified, be
produced within the plenitude of a present and absolute presence': *Of
Grammatology*, translated by Gayatri Spivak (Baltimore, MD: Johns
Hopkins University Press, 1976), p. 69.

'a conviction . . .'
Stephen Gill, *William Wordsworth: A Life* (Oxford: Clarendon Press,
1989), p. 154; Mary Jacobus in *Romanticism, Writing and Sexual Difference* also writes of *The Prelude* as a 'providential narrative on the singling
out of the individual mind as the privileged subject' (p. 73).

felix culpa
Gayatri Spivak in her essay on *The Prelude* in *In Other Worlds* notes that
'Many passages in these later books bring the French Revolution under

control by declaring it to be a *felix culpa*, a necessary means towards Wordsworth's growth as a poet . . . (p. 52).

'I was born . . .'
'Autobiographical Memoranda', *Prose Works*, vol. 3, p. 371.

73 *'Saturday'*
Dorothy Wordsworth, *Journals*, edited by Mary Moorman (Oxford: Oxford University Press, 1971), p. 106.

inconsequential listing of events
Writing about history-writing, Hayden White distinguishes between chronicle and historical narrative. Chronicle merely records in a list of items what has happened, historical narrative (as we understand it today) would (1) chain those listed events together in terms of cause and effect while (2) interpreting that causality as a teleology on the basis of a sense of what is typical about it. In *The Content of the Form* (Baltimore, MD: Johns Hopkins University Press, 1987), White asks 'What wish is enacted, what desire is gratified, by the fantasy that real events are properly represented when they can be shown to display the formal coherency of a story?' (p. 4). His answer, in crude summary, is a wish for mastery and social identity. To have the power to construct a narrative about its past enables a society to identify itself and where it's going by affirming the kind of ancestors it would like to have had.

74 'we seek . . .'
Freud, 'Screen Memories', *Standard Edition*, vol. 3, p. 303.

Narrativizing identity begins with the sentence.
See Lacan, *Ecrits*, p. 303.

prospectively . . . retrospectively
Ibid., p. 303.

I will have been
Lacan refers to the position of the subject as a 'retroversion effect' produced across the signifying chain so that the subject 'will have been' only 'in the future perfect tense' (ibid., p. 306).

'the unceasing present of enunciation'
Emile Benveniste, *Problèmes de linguistique générale*, 2 vols (Paris: Gallimard, 1974), vol. 2, p. 84.

75 we confess all the time.
'The confession . . . plays a part in justice, medicine, education, family relationship, and love relations, in the most ordinary affairs of everyday life, and in the most solemn rites . . .': Michel Foucault, *The History of Sexuality*, vol. 1: 'An Introduction' (Harmondsworth: Penguin, 1981), p. 59.

'empty speech'
Lacan, *Ecrits*, p. 42.

'I'm in words . . .'
Samuel Beckett, *The Unnameable* (New York: Grove Press, 1958),
p. 139. As Lacan says, 'I identify myself in language, but only by losing
myself in it like an object': *Ecrits*, p. 86.

76   'A Reader who has . . .'
William Wordsworth to Mrs. Clarkson, December 1814, cited in *Poetical
Works*, vol. 5, p. 464.

77   'I have said . . .'
Wordsworth, 'Preface' to *Lyrical Ballads*, *Poetical Works*, vol. 2,
pp. 400–401.

78   two people
M.H. Abrams in *Natural Supernaturalism: Tradition and Revolution in
Romantic Literature* (New York: Norton, 1971) cites this passage from
The Prelude and comments that there is a 'wide "vacancy" between the
I now and the I then' (p. 75).

subject of enounced/enunciation
See note to p. 35, above, p. 138.

79   'Personally of course . . .'
Samuel Beckett, *Watt* (London: John Calder, 1963), p. 44.

Operation Margarine
Roland Barthes, *Mythologies* (London: Paladin, 1972), pp. 41–2.

80   'an *identification*'
Freud, 'Mourning and Melancholia', *PFL*, vol. 11, p. 258. Freud discriminates between mourning and melancholia on the basis that in mourning, repetition leads to indifference, proving that it was a largely
conscious effect whereas in melancholia repetition reveals the object to
be charged, showing it was an unconscious effect.

a universe of lost objects
That the subject consists only of its attempt to make good its lost object
is suggested by Lacan when he writes: 'What is the subject? It is necessary
to find the subject as a lost object. More precisely, this lost object is
the support of the subject': 'Of Structure as an Inmixing of Otherness
Prerequisite to any Subject Whatever', in Richard Macksey and Eugenio
Donato (eds), *The Structuralist Controversy* (Baltimore, MA: Johns
Hopkins University Press, 1970), p. 189.

81   'successive evenings'
Coleridge arrived at the Wordsworth's on 21 December 1806 and the
poem was recited on various evenings 'shortly after': Gill, *William Wordsworth: A Life*, p. 255.

83   'to see himself seeing himself'
     For a discussion of 'I see myself seeing myself', see Lacan, *Four Fundamental Concepts*, p. 80.

85   *The Unnameable*
     Samuel Beckett (New York: Grove Press, 1958): 'I seem' (p. 3); 'all these' (p. 21); 'It's of me' (p. 51), 'I'm Worm' (p. 83).

86   'T' is past controversy . . .'
     Locke, *An Essay Concerning Human Understanding*, Book 4, Ch. 3, s. 6, p. 543; cited by Catherine Belsey, *The Subject of Tragedy* (London: Routledge, 1985), p. 84.

87   'Originally the ego . . .'
     Freud, *Civilisation and its Discontents*, PFL, vol. 12, p. 255; cited by Lionel Trilling, 'The Immortality Ode' (1941), *The Liberal Imagination* (New York: Anchor Books, 1953), pp. 124–54 at p. 140.

88   'I took hold . . .'
     Wordsworth to Mrs Fenwick, *The Poetical Works*, vol. 4, p. 464.

89   'this historical moment . . .'
     Lacan, *Four Fundamental Concepts*, p. 223.

     'I have resolved . . .'
     Jean-Jacques Rousseau, *The Confessions*, translated by J.M. Cohen (Harmondsworth: Penguin, 1953), p. 17.

6 Gender

91   Thomas Laqueur
     See *Making Sex: Body and Gender from the Greeks to Freud* (Cambridge, Mass.: Harvard University Press, 1990).

     '"I am the author"'
     Christine Battersby, *Gender and Genius: Towards a Feminist Aesthetics* (London: The Women's Press, 1989), p. 43.

92   'of all the men . . .'
     Coleridge, *The Table Talk and Omniana of Samuel Taylor Coleridge* edited by T. Ashe (London: York Library, 1905), p. 339.

     'Milton and Ben Jonson'
     Virginia Woolf, *A Room of One's Own* (London: Grafton, 1977), p. 99.

     'does not take place'
     Jacques Lacan, *Feminine Sexuality*, translated by Jacqueline Rose (London: Macmillan, 1982), p. 138 (the full quotation says that 'in the case of the speaking being the relation between the sexes does not take

place'). For a striking and original working through of Lacan's position, see Rob Lapsley and Michael Westlake, 'From *Casablanca* to *Pretty Woman*: The Politics of Romance', *Screen*, vol. 33, no. 1 (Spring, 1992), pp. 27–49.

be the phallus
See Lacan, 'The Signification of the Phallus', *Ecrits*, pp. 281–91.

'Woman [is] shut out'
Spivak, 'Sex and History in The Prelude', *In Other Worlds*, p. 57.

93   'son *and* lover'
Ibid., p. 47.

94   'Where they love . . .'
Freud, 'On the Universal Tendency to Debasement in the Sphere of Love', *PFL*, vol. 7, p. 251.

96   the attributes of a fetish
See Freud, 'Fetishism', *PFL*, vol. 7, pp. 345–58.

99   'does not use the word'
Marlon Ross, *The Contours of Masculine Desire*, p. 47.

'a rejection . . .'
Jacobus, *Romanticism, Writing and Sexual Difference*, p. 8.

it is everything and the other is nothing
Lacan proposes that the paradigm for aggression is 'I am nothing of what happens to me. You are nothing of value': *Ecrits*, p. 20.

100   'dread of women'
Freud, 'The Taboo of Virginity', *PFL*, vol. 7, p. 271.

'the male unconscious . . .'
Laura Mulvey, 'Visual Pleasure and Narrative Cinema', *Screen*, vol. 16, no. 3 (Summer 1975), pp. 6–18, 13–14.

102   'love is essentially deception . . .'
Lacan, *Four Fundamental Concepts*, p. 268.

103   her otherness is reduced
In the course of analysing the 'male mastery' of the 'Lucy' poem, 'A slumber did my spirit seal', J. Hillis Miller writes that the text treats its subject in a way which 'recapitulates in reverse mirror image the action of the early years in touching, penetrating, possessing, killing, encompassing, turning the other into oneself and therefore being left only with a corpse, an empty sign': *Romanticism and Contemporary Criticism*, p. 108.

104   'earthly years'
'To be touched by earthly years is a way to be sexually penetrated while still remaining a virgin'; Hillis Miller, ibid., p. 107.

'the poem is written'
de Man, *Blindness and Insight*, 2nd edn, pp. 224–5. Actually, de Man continues in a way that must incur some reticence, for he appears to dismiss his own acknowledgment that it is an ideological condition for the dead person to be a woman on the grounds that Wordsworth could – and did – write about his own death. Here he is relapsing into the usual critical elision between the historical author and the Wordsworth in the texts; only the reader in the present can now produce Wordsworth's death – he can only speak from beyond the grave because a speaking subject enables him to.

105   'To make . . .'
Sarah Kofman, *The Enigma of Woman*, translated by Catherine Porter (Ithaca, NY: Cornell University Press, 1985), p. 223.

'The only safe woman . . .'
Leslie Fiedler, *Love and Death in the American Novel* (London: Paladin, 1970), p. 249. The full quotation reads: 'To save the female for polite readers who wanted women but not sex was not an easy matter. The only safe woman . . .'.

7 Language

106   'With this goes . . .'
Caudwell, *Illusion and Reality*, p. 93.

Prince Genji
Michael Westlake, *51 Sōkō To the Islands on the Other Side of the World* (Edinburgh: Polygon, 1990).

107   Wordsworth believes that language
W.J.T. Mitchell gives a fine account of Wordsworth's sense of the difference between speech and writing in 'Visible Language', in *Romanticism and Contemporary Criticism*, pp. 46–95.

'Words are too awful . . .'
Wordsworth, 'Essay on Epitaphs', *Prose Works*, vol. 2, pp. 84–5.

'in expressing what . . .'
Wordsworth, 'Preface' to *Lyrical Ballads*, *Poetical Works*, vol. 2, p. 393.

'poetry is . . .'
Ibid., p. 387.

'neither is . . .'
Ibid., p. 392.

108   'fall short . . .'
Ibid., p. 394.

'However, exalted . . .'
Ibid., p. 394 ('exalted', 1845; 'his situation is altogether slavish and mechanical', 1802–1832; 1836 omits altogether).

'Why, professing . . .'
Ibid., p. 398.

'superadd . . . charm'
Ibid., p. 398.

113   'a certain colouring of imagination . . .'
Ibid., p. 386.

'to the action and situation . . .'
Ibid., p. 389.

'a repetition . . .'
Coleridge, *Biographia Literaria*, vol. 1, p. 202. If you read the whole page, you'll appreciate why, as a student, I got lost in this kind of thing.

'Subjectivity expands . . .'
Belsey, *Literature, Politics and Theory*, p. 74.

'a Poet's *Heart* . . .'
Coleridge, letter to Sotheby (10 September 1802), *Collected Letters of Samuel Taylor Coleridge*, vol. 2, p. 459.

'to transfer . . .'
Coleridge, *Biographia Literaria*, vol. 2, p. 6.

114   'images, however beautiful . . .'
Ibid., p. 16.

116   'When Wordsworth . . .'
Charles Taylor, *Sources of Self: The Making of Modern Identity* (Cambridge: Cambridge University Press, 1989), p. 381.

'a projection . . .'
Williams, *The Country and the City*, p. 166.

118   the *fort/da* game
See Freud, *Beyond the Pleasure Principle*, PFL, vol. 11, pp. 283–7. This describes a little boy of a year and a half playing a version of the familiar child's game of lost and found; he had a reel with a piece of string tied round it and would repeat the game of throwing the reel away while making a sound equivalent to *fort* (German: gone), then pulling it back with a sound equivalent to *da* (there).

120   act of mourning
See Lacan, 'Desire and the Interpretation of Desire in Hamlet', *Yale French Studies*, vols 55–6, pp. 11–52.

syntactical organisation
The potential for syntagmatic closure to exercise control was referred to earlier in another context (see p. 74).

'a *matter-of-factness*'
Coleridge, *Biographia Literaria*, vol. 2, p. 101.

121   'Surprised by joy'
Though probably motivated for William Wordsworth by the death of his daughter, Catherine, at the age of three, the sonnet actually reads as though it were addressed to a mature partner, almost in fact like a 'Lucy' poem.

122   'it is the world of words . . .'
Lacan, *Ecrits*, p. 65.

8 The Heart of a Heartless World

123   τοῦ λογου
Heraclitus, fragment, cited by T.S. Eliot as an epigraph for 'Burnt Norton'.

124   'Like a Prayer'
From 'The Immaculate Collection: Madonna' (1990), © Sire Records 1990, Warner Music.

126   'isolation of the individual'
Frederick Engels, *The Condition of the Working Class in England* (London: Granada, 1969), p. 58.

'private, enclosed'
Williams, *The Country and City*, p. 356.

127   'the self-creating . . .'
Robert Langbaum, *The Mysteries of Identity: A Theme in Modern Literature* (New York: Oxford University Press, 1977), p. 47.

'the philosophical cogito'
Lacan, *Ecrits*, p. 165.

Index

THE POLITICS OF PLEASURE
AESTHETICS AND CULTURAL THEORY

Stephen Regan

For many years the study of aesthetics was regarded as a narrow and limited preoccupation, having only the slightest social and political relevance. With the advent of deconstruction, aesthetic considerations came to be seen not just as unfashionable but as deeply suspect and reprehensible. Within the growing realm of cultural studies, however, there is a strong and sustained revival of interest in questions of pleasure and value. The essays in this volume constitute a radical recovery and reappraisal of aesthetics and insist upon the continuing significance of aesthetic issues in modern culture. They address Marxist and feminist aesthetics, aesthetics and literary theory, modernism and postmodernism, pleasure and value. As well as surveying the aesthetic theories of Walter Pater, Roger Fry, Clive Bell, I.A. Richards, Roland Barthes, Paul de Man and others, these essays offer new and provocative interpretations of specific works of art. Among the writers whose works are discussed are William Wordsworth, Charles Baudelaire, Virginia Woolf, Franz Kafka, Samuel Beckett and Doris Lessing. Together, these essays welcome the return of the aesthetic as a powerful and productive idea in contemporary cultural politics.

Contents

Contributors

Michèle Barrett, Laurel Brake, Steven Connor, Terry Eagleton, Robin Jarvis, Adrian Page, Stephen Regan, Rebecca Stott, Geoff Wade, Patricia Waugh.

240 pp   0 335 09759 6 (Paperback)

RHYTHM AND RHYME

Ronald Tamplin

Although metre is clearly one of the most important distinguishing features of poetry, it is often perceived as an arcane area and merely technical in its importance. Ron Tamplin breathes fresh life into discussion of rhythm and rhyme by considering their meanings as well as their manifestations, and by examining how metrical changes parallel social and cultural shifts. On one level he argues in favour of very simple descriptions of metrical patterns (rather than endless technical discussion of metrical nuances); on another, he argues that rhythm is a prime means of structuring experience and that the patterns of poetry are as 'natural' as they are 'artificial'.

Contents

Analysing rhythm and rhyme – The meaning of poetic patterns – Patterns in use: before the twentieth century – Patterns in use: twentieth-century verse methods – Why patterns change: the fourteenth and sixteenth centuries – Why patterns change: from classical to romantic – Particularities and patternings – Glossary – Notes – Suggestions for further reading – Index.

128pp   0 335 09451 1 (Paperback)   0 335 09452 X (Hardback)

THE PRELUDE

Nigel Wood (ed.)

The Prelude, in its several unpublished forms as well as its printed 1850 edition, is often taken to offer an insight into Wordsworth's own life as well as the events that most affected it, including the French Revolution and the subjective implications of the Romantic sublime. Recent scholarship has provided the reader with a much altered Wordsworth and fresh perspectives on the ideology of Romanticism. This volume of specially commissioned essays contains examples of how the newest critical positions, often taught in separate courses, may be brought to bear in practice on *The Prelude*. Sections in each essay locate a context for the theories adopted and explain any unfamiliar terms. There then follows an interpretation of the work guided by these theoretical concepts. An introduction from the volume editor supplies an account of the critical history of the poem and an explanation of its textual situation (and how it affects the work of interpretation). This also provides an overview of the most recent criticism on Wordsworth and some indication of how these have affected the practical approaches to his work.

Contents
Editor's preface – Preface – How to use this book – A note on the text – Introduction – Paul de Man and imaginative consolation – Romantic space: topo-analysis and subjectivity – Working The Prelude: *Foucault and the New History – 'Answering questions and questioning answers': the interrogative project – Endpiece – Notes – References – Further reading – Index.*

Contributors
Jon Cook, Philip Shaw, Clifford Siskin, Susan Wolfson, Nigel Wood.

224pp   0 335 09626 3 (Paperback)